WHITE
SOUL

WHITE SOUL

Country Music, the Church, and Working Americans

TEX SAMPLE

Abingdon Press
Nashville

WHITE SOUL:
COUNTRY MUSIC, THE CHURCH, AND WORKING AMERICANS

Copyright © 1996 by Abingdon Press

This book is printed on acid-free, recycled paper.

Library of Congress Cataloging-in-Publication Data

Sample, Tex.
  White soul : country music, the Church, and working Americans/
Tex Sample.
    p.   cm.
  Includes index.
  ISBN 0-687-03293-8 (alk. paper)
  1. Country music—Social aspects. 2. Music and society—United States. 3. Working class whites—United States. 4. Church and labor—United States. I. Title.
  ML3524.S26   1996
  781.642—dc20   96-18231
                                                       CIP

Scripture quotations are from the New Revised Standard Version Bible, copyright © 1989 by the Division of Christian Education of the National Council of the Churches of Christ in the USA.

96 97 98 99 00 01 02 03 04 05 — 10 9 8 7 6 5 4 3 2 1

MANUFACTURED IN THE UNITED STATES OF AMERICA

To
Patricia Ann Sample Smith
and
Shelby "Chuck" Smith

Contents

Contents

Part Four: The Implications for the Church

Acknowledgments

Nothing makes me more self-consciously aware of how indebted I am than the writing of a book. It is not only the academic debt, but also the personal and the autobiographical, the relational and the happenstance, and the coming around of things you think you rejected long ago and suddenly begin to understand in new ways. Here I can mention but a few of those who helped me see country music as White Soul.

My mother loved country music. Because her country music was the sound on the radio as I came to consciousness every morning during my early years, I owe Mama.

Larry Don Hollon and I have taught a course on country music and working people for twenty years. I can no longer tell how much he taught me, except to say that there is nothing I think about in the music in which I cannot hear his voice in the conversation. He also gave the manuscript a careful reading.

Over the past seven years my conversations and correspondence with Stanley Hauerwas have been of central importance in addressing the range of practices among working people and country music. My appreciation for his work and for his friendship overwhelms my traditional resistance as a Mississippian to Texans. His reading of the manuscript was especially helpful in the encouragement to keep my story and "voice" present throughout.

We get by with help from our friends, and I still don't know how I manage to have such good ones. The following read part or all of the manuscript: Debra Bendis, Eugene Lowry, Fran Manson, Judith Orr, and Emilie Townes. I only wish I were able to take greater advantage of all their comments.

I believe that I would never have focused on working people and country music if I had not taught at Saint Paul School of Theology. It is not only the freedom of the place; but also the central concern there to serve the church. More than that, I simply cannot imagine any other institution putting up with me so patiently for nearly thirty years. More specifically, I am grateful to the trustees, administration, faculty, staff, and students for the sabbatical leave in the fall semester of 1995 during which time this book was written.

To Dean R. Kevin LaGree of the Candler School of Theology at Emory University I am indebted for the invitation to give The Quillian Lectures in 1994. It was there that I developed for the first time what appears as chapters 5 and 6 on the contradictions of country music. I also thank the Oklahoma School of Ministry of The United Methodist Church for their invitation to lecture there in 1994. With them I formulated what appears throughout the book as a critique of elitist taste.

Kathleen Campbell has worked faithfully and carefully as a research assistant with me for over ten years. Her contribution is substantial and not measurable. Theresa Mastrogiovanni was my student assistant for the academic year 1994–95. She chased down and dug out journal articles and bibliographies. Margaret Kohl, faculty secretary at Saint Paul, was a cordial worker with floppy disks and other things related to the computer.

My sister, Patricia, had the good sense to love country music all her life, unlike her brother who went through "an uppity time." She also had the good sense to marry Chuck Smith. Both of them are lifelong country music fans. This book is dedicated to them.

I must also express indebtedness to the woman I love. Fortunately, I'm married to her. She turns ordinary time into a liturgy of friendship and punctuates it with the litanies of affection. Because of her I understand what it means to sing "I'd waltz across Texas with you."

Introduction
White Soul

Third-party presidential candidate George Wallace was making a speech at a rally in Kansas City. A number of us were there passing out leaflets to attenders refuting charges he had made in previous stump speeches. The women in our group wore business-style dresses, and the men were dressed in suits and ties. At first, people who took the leaflets from us thought we were supporting Wallace. They smiled and remarked how nice we looked. As they walked on by and read it, however, they became quite angry. Some wadded up the paper and returned to throw it at us.

Standing there I remember being strangely disturbed. Not by their animosity, not even by being hit with the leaflets—rocks scare me, not paper wads. What really bothered me was that I thought I "knew" the people who attended the rally. They were the people I had known all my life. Most of them were working-class folks: my people, my kin, and, in a very real sense, me!

The overwhelming mass of working people did not support George Wallace and certainly did not vote for him. But in that moment of observing working-class people at this rally, I realized that I had lost touch with my own people. I simply did not know them.

While growing up in Mississippi, my earliest memories of my father were in the Great Depression when he worked as an iceman, a cobbler, and a school bus driver. Later, he would be a sheet metal worker in the shipyards of New Orleans during World War II. With the money from that he bought a small cafe in McComb, and a year later traded that for a small cab-stand back in Brookhaven. I had started answering the phone there when I was about twelve and could write down addresses. Later, I drove a cab while in high school. During college I worked summers in construction and in the oil fields. In graduate study I served a small working-class church in Haverhill, Massachusetts. But somehow through four years of college, three years of seminary, four years in a Ph.D. program, and then three years as a social action executive for the Massachusetts Council of Churches, and then as a first-year professor in a theological school, I realized that I was no longer in touch with the very people from whom I came.

As I left the arena that evening I made a promise to myself that I would begin the very next day to find out all I could about working people. Ever since it has been the primary focus of my research and study. I also sought out the people. I played football for two seasons on a working-class church team until I got too old. I sought out softball teams where working-class men made up most of the players, playing on those for nearly twenty years. I became more intentional about keeping up my friendships with working people and sought out working-class settings like honky-tonks to spend my leisure time. Along the way I developed a relationship with an AA motorcycle gang through my son Steve. Since my other son, Shawn, is a working guy and my daughter, Jennifer, is a hairdresser, I began to pay attention to them in new ways. Students who came out of working-class families became a special interest in my teaching, and I developed courses that attempted to be sensitive to class issues as well as to those of gender and race.

I had rejected country music when I was still in grammar school. I got involved in a rhythm band and later took up the cornet and was taught "good music." In efforts to reacquaint myself with working people I soon realized that alienation from my roots had its beginnings there. In the mid-1970s, conversations with my friend Larry Don Hollon helped me realize how important country music is to working-class life. Out of that he and I began teaching a course on country music and working Americans at Saint Paul School of Theology. We have taught that course for twenty years. This book represents what I have learned.

Finally, I come to this work as a Christian and as a church person. I am very concerned that the church is losing its relation to working people in the United States. The class captivity of the church seems to be increasing, and not only among more upper status established churches. As much as anything I can accomplish in this book, I want to change this situation. My central concern is to understand the lives of working people so that the church can engage in an indigenous ministry with them that takes their practices, their struggles, and their wisdom with the utmost seriousness. Basic to this concern is an opposition to the inequalities of class and the search for a church committed to social justice. The final section of the book is devoted to this search.

Country Music and Working People

It is not my contention that all working people like country music or that all fans of country music are working class. Such claims would not be true. I do maintain that country music has primarily been the soul music of rural and urban white working people across most of the twentieth century. Support for such a view is quite strong. Tony Scherman says that country music "charted the vicissitudes of working class life."[1] Bill Malone, who has written the definitive study of the history of country music, observes that country performers and their core audience have been working people, who are "locked too often in dead-end jobs that offer neither fulfillment nor security, and living in an American society that values neither working people nor work unless glamorous or status related."[2] Mary A. Bufwack and Robert K. Oermann, who have done the most comprehensive study of the role of women in country music, contend that country music is the "songs and styles of the working class." By quoting Tillie Olsen they maintain that country music is the music of "our silenced people." These are the people, says Olsen, who for ages are "consumed in the hard, everyday essential work of maintaining human life."[3]

13

Some might argue that the music is mainly a Southern phenomenon. While it had its origins in the Southeast in the twenties, it moved quickly to the Southwest in the thirties. During the late thirties and especially during World War II, it became a national, and eventually an international, music. In the second half of the twentieth century it circled the globe with country music ventures in places as different as Germany and Japan.

It is also true that the music increasingly reaches a much wider audience than working people alone. This is due in part to the efforts of the country music industry itself to "cross over" into the wider popular market. *American Demographics* reports that country music is now listened to by 60 percent of all Americans. According to the Donnelleys's Cluster-Plus system used by Arbitron, it is "the most popular radio format in the U.S." and 40 percent of country's fans are in the three most affluent groups of listeners.[4] Clearly, the effort to expand the audience of country music is working, so much so that some observers of the music question whether it will sustain its identity in the pressure of such crossover success.[5]

This means that country music itself is becoming more diverse. Within the music, however, is a significant core that from its beginning and throughout its history embodies working-class life with all its sense of loss, dislocation, alienation, celebration, defiance, holding on, making it, and hope. My intent is to examine mainly the songs and artists who have represented the heart of the music, which addresses working-class life.

White Soul

This dominant core of the music is what I refer to as White Soul.[6] By calling it White Soul, my purpose is to focus on country music and white working people. I hope this focus will not be misunderstood. It is my intent to recognize the particularity of white working-class life, and by that, not to assume that such a study addresses all working people, but to underscore the diversity of U.S. life and to challenge views that tend to assume tacitly that America is "white" and that other views are peripheral. Rather, we have a mosaic of racial-ethnic groups in this country, and we need to speak more specifically of each of them. One way to do this is to look carefully, both critically and appreciatively, at the soul music of our various communities. My life and my study prepare me to speak about the people from which I came. Representatives of other groups are more than prepared to address the lives and stories of their own communities.

By White Soul I also mean to convey that country music bears the "essence" of white working life. By "essence," I do not mean an ideal characteristic working itself out in history (in some Hegelian sense), but that the music reflects and embodies the lived lives of white working people. It sings their stories, displays their emotions, manifests their tastes, struggles with their spirituality, speaks to the structure of their work, names the vulnerabilities and celebrations of their loves, keeps their memories warm, faces the contradictions of their lives, and yearns for tomorrows without the hardship and desperation of dead-end jobs, tight money, and the constant fight to make it and get by. The music is a forum for the articulation of resistance to a dominant world where their lives, their ways, and their dignity are constantly under attack. Often accused of being apolitical or at the very least "conservative," I shall argue instead that it embodies a traditional politics with anarchistic overtones of a populist sort. All of these things point to country music as embodying white working-class life in its rich diversity. It is White Soul.

To suggest that country music is soul is not to deny that it is subjected to a relentless commercialization. Because of this some contend that the music does not so much reflect the lives of working people as it generates feelings and desires in consumerist directions. While it would be naive to believe that the culture industry is impotent to affect the lives of the public, I maintain that it is not enough to examine what the country music industry does. One must also explore the ways that working people themselves use country music. This is a basic aim of this work.

Working People

Who are these working people? A popular view in this society is that the blue-collar worker is no longer a major part of our national life because we are increasingly a postindustrial and info-technological society in a global economy. While factory workers no longer occupy as dominant a place among workers as they once did, nevertheless working-class occupations still constitute a large number of workers in the United States. It is true that the occupational structure has changed radically across this century and continues to do so, and the impact of a global economy is pervasive and is changing the shape of life in this society and around the world. Such changes, however, have by no means eliminated the working American. They are more diverse, but certainly not less present.

In the mid-nineties the U.S. has almost 13.7 million precision production, craft, and repair workers, 18.4 million operators, fabricators, and laborers, and 16.9 million service occupations, the overwhelming majority of which are working class. These add up to 49 million workers in a total of a 124.7 million occupations in the U.S.[7] Working people are hardly disappearing![8] What's more, other occupations can be seen as having a significant proportion of their workers as working class, especially if one sees these as downscale jobs that are dull, monotonous, routine, and repetitive. For example, a large proportion of secretarial jobs are as much like factory jobs in terms of their heavily structured, routinized character and the close supervision of the worker's performance.

One result of the economic changes in the U.S. is what economist Wallace Peterson calls "the silent depression," an economic reversal experienced by millions of Americans. Beginning in 1973, this "silent depression" is characterized by a decline in the rate of growth of the real income of the average worker and real median family income, a rising rate of unemployment, a growing gap between the rich and the poor, a declining "Index of Social Health"—factors like infant mortality, child abuse, drug abuse, and unemployment—"a decade of greed and economic mismanagement," tremendous increases in the U.S. deficit and indebtedness, and political commitments controlled by a powerful corporate and political oligarchy.[9]

One very clear illustration of this silent depression is the loss of pay by American workers. Average hourly earnings among private sector employees was $7.41 through October 1995, in constant 1982 dollars. This is down form $8.55 in those same constant dollars in 1973. This represents more than a 13 percent loss in average hourly earnings across this period of time.[10] This deterioration is especially pronounced among white working men as we shall see below.

One must not forget the unemployed in this silent depression. In late 1995, the Bureau of Labor Statistics reports that 1.4 million (7.7 percent) service workers, 715,000 (5.0 percent) precision production, craft, and repair workers and 1.4 million (7.1 percent) operators, fabricators, and laborers were officially unemployed.[11] But this figure does not include 4.9 million workers who are employed part-time but want full-time work. In addition there are 7.3 million "discouraged workers," people who want work but are not actively pursuing it, although 1.7 million of these did seek employment during the past year.[12] These figures add up to 20 million people!

Moving from occupational categories to households, one gets yet another striking picture of economic reversal. Jan Larson reports in *American Demographics* that 43 percent of, or 40 million, U.S. households make less than $25,000 a year, which is what she terms "downscale." (One-fourth of all households had incomes under $15,000 in 1989.) Eighty-one percent of the "downscale" households are white, 16 percent are black (representing 11 percent of all households), and 8 percent are Hispanic (representing 6 percent of all households). These downscale households are more likely to be young or old, with the former struggling to make it and the old living on fixed incomes. They are less likely to live in families or to be married, although 35 percent are married couples, compared with 56 percent of all households.[13] Eighteen percent of these downscale households are single women heads of families. Of these downscale workers, 2 million full-time workers are poor. In forty-five states, two full-time minimum wage workers "would not earn enough to be able to afford the average rent for a two bedroom apartment in 1989."[14]

Moreover, wages below poverty rose from 25.7 percent to 31.5 percent of wage earners from 1979 to 1987. These poor workers got poorer at the same time that executive salaries soared, according to Barbara Ehrenreich in *Time* magazine. While union workers make 30 percent more than nonunion, only 16.1 percent of the work force was organized in 1991.[15] The good news is that an upturn occurred in 1993, when 200,000 new members joined unions, the first increase in fourteen years.[16] In this time of silent depression the earnings for women continue to be well below those of men, that is, white men. In service occupations and in the category of operators, fabricators, and laborers, the median incomes of women are a little over 74 percent of those of men. In the more skilled category of precision production, craft, and repair this figure drops to a little over 64 percent. Across all wage and salary workers women have median incomes that are 75.6 percent of those of men. It does not take much imagination to see what happens to a single woman in these occupations, especially if she has children.[17]

Among white women and racial-ethnics the earnings of black males are nearly commensurate with those of white women, but the earnings of Hispanic males trail those of both these groups, matching almost exactly the earnings of black females in 1995. Hispanic females fall behind all of these.[18] It is clear that white men fare far better than white women and racial-ethnic men and women. At the same time, in the working-class world the majority of none of these groups is doing well.

It is also clear that there are higher rates of poverty for white women and racial-ethnic men and women in the United States. At the same time, white men in sheer numbers are the second largest group of adults in the society who are poor, next to white women. Moreover, in a discussion of trends during the eighties Michael Harrington points out that the closing of the distance between the wages of white working men and those of white women and racial-ethnic men and women is the result of the decrease of the wages of white men and not of substantive gains by these two other groups. He argues that the future of racial-ethnic men and women and white women is presaged by the fate of the white working man: "Today's white male misery is a deadly prediction of worse times for women and minorities."[19] In a more recent study, Sam Roberts finds that "the narrower gap [between women's and men's earnings] was less a reflection of progress by women than of a decline in men's earnings."[20]

This picture becomes more dreary when one looks at the impact of the new technological-informational industries. Jane Bryant Quinn reports on a study by the Economic Policy Institute that between 1979 and 1994 "the average hourly earnings dropped 28 percent for males who didn't finish high school, 16 percent for high school graduates, and 11 percent for those who put in some college time." Quinn further reports that while real family incomes rose during most of the 1980s, they did so because more wives took jobs. Meanwhile, during the decade 1983–1993, 20 million new jobs were added, but these tended to be distributed at the two ends of the occupational and income spectrum. That is, more high wage jobs like those of technicians and professionals were generated at one end and more low wage hourly worker jobs at the other, with fewer jobs in the middle. Furthermore, she reports that in July of 1995, an American Management Association survey found that 29.5 percent of the companies intended to cut their work force in the next year, but the AMA expected this figure to be closer to 60 percent. The good news is that these companies hired as many people as they fired in 1994 to 1995, but the pattern of terminations and employment does not favor working-class people. Quinn maintains that "the prime cause of wage inequality appears to be technological change." This suggests that the effects of these technological changes will fall heavily and disproportionately on the working class.[21]

There are more data, but enough here to say that there are serious financial problems in the U.S. working class, whatever the race or gender. In the light of these kinds of economic conditions, the country song makes a lot of sense when it contends that there is "too much month at the end of the money."[22]

Working-class people are not disappearing and millions experience a silent depression. Many are poor and near poor. Moreover, the plight of the white working man is real. That his lot is a better one than that of other workers is hardly happy news when his situation is deteriorating and indeed marks the loss of good working-class jobs in the society, a reality with fateful portent for all working women and racial-ethnic men.

Further, the struggle of working-class white women, especially with changes in family and household structure, is an even more dreary picture. It is not necessary, nor is it my intention, to minimize or be complacent about the severe circumstances of racial-ethnic men and women and the racism this represents. The last thing we need in this society is competition about whose situation is worse among the poor, the near poor, and the downwardly mobile. What is needed are changes in the racist, sexist, and class patterns of a society that seems increasingly uncaring about the people who finally make the society work.

The focus here is on the white working class and country music, not because I will avoid the issues of racism, but because I want to address primarily the issues of white working Americans and because I believe that no music captures their lives like that of country music. Their financial hardships, struggles with bosses, the work they do, their excitement about romantic love and the lament of its loss, their patriotism and distrust of government, the incongruities of their existence, their resistance to the institutions and cultural values that demean their lifestyles, and their spiritualities and conflicts with the church can all be found in the music.

An Overview of the Book

In what follows I examine this range of issues in the relationship between country music and white working people. Such issues emerge from the dynamics of inequality. They permeate white working-class life and the music.

To address these I have divided the book into four parts.

The first deals with the question of taste. Most of the objections one hears to country music come as expressions of taste. Pierre Bourdieu maintains that taste is basically defined by disgust. That is, one's taste is often established by what one cannot stand.[23] The comment we hear is that "it makes me sick." Such things open up an array of questions. What is it about country music that makes people ill? My conviction is that the more lower class it is, the more disgust it creates among its detractors. When I encounter such reactions, I get suspicious. If issues of class draw miasmal symptoms, I cannot help wondering if a politics is at work. I argue precisely this in part I.

Chapter 1 begins this discussion with a contrast between lower-class taste and upper-class or elitist taste. I suggest here something of the historical and social origins of these two forms and offer the view that country music embodies working-class taste, at least in its best work. In chapter 2 this discussion continues and demonstrates the role that taste plays in a politics of inequality.

Issues of taste inevitably bring questions about how one grounds or establishes "good taste." That is, how do we know what is good taste and what isn't? This is the concern of part II. In chapter 3 I argue that there is no known way to establish the supremacy of a particular musical tradition. Rather, the standards of good music develop in their various traditions and are specific to them. The practices of these traditions develop criteria of "critical" judgment, "trained" participation, and "informed" appreciation. (I place "critical," "learned," and "informed" in quotes because I do not want to suggest that such standards necessarily require development in institutions of higher education.)

Such traditions serve certain goods, and judgments about the quality of their achievements emerge and are refined in the development of these traditions. In chapter 4 I discuss the goods that country music serves and suggest that standards of quality develop from the practices that are intrinsic to these goods. The central good of country music is its embodiment of the lives of rural and urban workers. In this chapter I name a number of the dimensions of this central good. For those who wish to read a history of country music, I have included a brief overview in the appendix, which focuses on the relation of the music to working people across the twentieth century.

Part III moves into a closer discussion of the music's embodiment of working-class lives. It focuses on two major dimensions of the working world that permeate the music: the contradictions of their lives, and their everyday resistance to the dominant order. In chapter 5 I examine the contradictions between tradition and modernity and between a traditional morality and "the wild side of life." In chapter 6 the focus turns to the contradictions of defiance and submission, the centrality and vulnerability of romantic love, sexism and the salvific role of women, and the important place of African Americans in country music and the virtual silence of the music about racism.

Chapter 7 argues that resistance plays a significant role in country music, so much so that I believe it can appropriately be called a politics. The focus is on the practices of this resistance and the way these are displayed in country music. It can best be named "everyday resistance." This chapter delineates a number of ways these practices are spelled out in the music and in working lives. In chapter 8 I attempt to describe the politics of this resistance as a traditional one that takes the form of a populist anarchism. This politics varies from the conventional left/middle/right continuum in this country and needs to be understood on other grounds. Any attempt to respond to the lived lives of working people that takes them seriously will come to terms with this political stance.

Part IV has three concerns. First, it asks how the church can respond to working people and the issues raised so far. Can it be a place of welcome to working people? Can the church deal with its own class captivity? Can it join with working people to challenge the contradictions of their lives? If so, how? In chapter 9 I propose that the church join the resistance of working people and become a community of resistance. Second, chapter 10 broaches the outlines of what such a church would look like and how it would address the important questions of spirituality, faith, and witness with working people. Such ministry needs country music as an important resource. Finally, chapter 11 examines the process of doing theology with country music and provides examples of this using the music. But before coming to the concerns of later chapters, such a ministry must first come to grips with the issue of taste and its political implications.

PART I

The Politics of Taste

Chapter 1

Rowdy and Loud
at the Twist and Shout:
Working-Class Taste

eggy and I lived in Boston for ten years. While there we developed a friendship with Joe and Mary, two fine people. Both came from wealthy families, and Joe's family was especially so. Joe was also a socially responsible young man. He was actively involved in the Civil Rights movement and the anti–Vietnam War effort. He put his body and his money where his mouth was. I deeply appreciated him.

The four of us went to a performance of *La Bohème* one night. Puccini is my favorite composer, and *La Bohème* is the work of his I love most. In the opera, a duet is sung by Mimi and Rodolfo shortly after their first meeting. Rodolfo intentionally knocks over the light, making it look like an accident so that he can make a play for Mimi's affection. Both of them are on the floor searching in the dark for the light, when he touches her hand and begins what I believe to be one of the most rapturous moments in the history of Western music. He begins singing the line [English translation]: "Your hand is cold." It is a magnificently beautiful duet.

When it comes to opera and symphonies, I am a classical music Pentecostal. I could not sit still. I began to move, pat my feet, and mimic the conductor while at the same time attempting to suppress my beatific convulsion. (The problem with most classical music is that the conductor is the only one who gets to cut up.) I was twitching and jerking, holding my breath one moment and bursting out with sighs and glossolalia-like expressions the next. Peggy elbowed me and told me that I was shaking the whole row. I was having an aesthetic conniption, a "hyperventilated" ecstatic orgasm, a mystical, spiritual apprehension of "the eternal." Had I put it in a country music idiom, I might have said that I was so carried away that "my eyes were all bugged out like a stomped on toad frog."

The duet ended with Rodolfo and Mimi bringing resolution to it by virtually shouting "Amor!" "Amor!" and then "Ah!" The first time they sang "Amor," it was just too much. You think you cannot stand anything so beautiful and so moving. Then they go farther up the scale, and shout again, "Amor," and the vocal focus and artistic statement avoid distortion of sound on the one hand and convey a heart-bursting ecstasy through the tonal and harmonic signs of this fresh, young love, on the other. By the time they came to the final "Ah!" I was emotionally a line of wrung-out washed clothes hanging in a windstorm of musical power.

As the audience came to its feet, I was shouting, whistling, and clapping as loudly and as vigorously as I could. I looked over at Joe. His face was a picture of emotionless calm; there was no contortion of body or countenance. While he was standing, his applause was the kind of light patter a businessperson might give at a Rotary Club meeting upon learning that his chief competitor had been named "Citizen of the Year."

"Joe, didn't you like it?" I asked, stunned by his absence of cathectic involvement.

"I thought it was extremely well done," he answered in such an uninvolved manner that I distinctly remember thinking that he would be emotionally flat at his own wedding.

"Did you really like it?" I asked, trying again, because his affect had all the repose of death.

"Oh, I thought the voice control and the blend of the soprano and the tenor were exquisitely done. The last progressions were especially effective. It was a superlative performance." All these things he said without overt feeling, the way someone might read a phone book.

Upper-Class and Elitist Taste: Distance, Detachment, Disinterestedness, and Indifference

In this vignette we have the expression of two basic forms of artistic taste that are deeply related to class. In Joe we have the manifestation of a classic style of upper-class or elitist taste. In my actions and response we find a working-class display. Sorting out the characteristics of these two styles is basic to all that follows. It divulges fundamental issues about taste and class and the character of country music. From a single event, like the opera and individuals' responses to it, we can begin to understand why country music is the soul music of so many working people in the United States.

Not all wealthy people have taste and express it as Joe does. Nor do all working-class people exhibit a style of taste the way I responded at the opera. There are, of course, diversities among the rich and the elites and among working people of any society, so far as I can tell. But Joe does manifest a form and style of taste that has been around for centuries, and my own style of expression has been evident among the working class for centuries, too.

Joe expresses his aesthetic taste in an upper-class style that has been well documented and carefully articulated and advanced by elites for some time. His approach derives from an understanding of art that is more distant and detached than my own. His manner is more disinterested and indifferent to the emotional impact of music on someone like me. The approach is a taste in art for the sake of art alone. This taste derives pleasure from art, but it is pleasure of a subjective kind, derived purely from the art itself; that is, it is not employed to engender emotional remonstrances such as I "exhibited" at the opera. In this elitist view the pleasure found is an intrinsically aesthetic one and hence requires no such classical pentecostal expressivism as mine. It is therefore more casual, and the response is more "cool"—I would, in an unsensitive moment, say lifeless—as Joe expressed it.

Joe's form of elitist taste is not eternal. Immanuel Kant (1724–1804) developed one of the most sophisticated arguments for this view of aesthetics in his *Critique of Judgment*. Kant proposes that art, or the aesthetic, should be understood as an end in itself. Its purpose is intrinsic. It is not a means to anything else—not ethical values or religion or hedonism. Kant says it is "a purposeless purposefulness." Since its only purpose is aesthetic it serves no utilitarian aim, no matter how good it is and regardless of its makeup.[1]

This view of aesthetics is often a matter of no little conflict in many communities. When citizen groups raise questions with art works that display nudity or sexual activity, or that do not have "socially redeeming value" or do not seem to mean anything, they will inevitably be countered by elitist art groups who wonder why such a question is raised at all. They contend that art is art for the sake of art, and is not to be held to criteria external to it, not even moral ones.[2] Such views of art and music have a primary indebtedness to Kant's work.

Moreover, this form of elitist and upper-class taste and style is not lost on working people. Note how often the taste is given a physically constrained and disembodied character in working-class language, such as when elites are called "tight-assed," or described as quite distanced from things of the body. A favorite expression of working men about a person with such taste is one who is so disembodied that he or she does not "know whether to shit or go blind."[3]

A "genteel" expression of these things can be found in the musical *Carousel*, where Billy Bigelow, a working-class barker at a carousel falls in love with Julie, a young woman who works at the mill. He has been a circus ne'er-do-well, but when he discovers that Julie is pregnant by him, he determines to change his life, and in the song "Soliloquy," he sings of his hopes for his son yet to be born—who turns out to be a she. At one point the lyric states "And I'll be damned if he'll marry the boss's daughter, a skinny lipped lady with blood like water, who'll give him a peck and call it a kiss, and look down her nose through a lorgnette."[4] Notice the lifeless, bloodless, erotic flatness of the boss's daughter. Note too the charge against a haughtiness and a disdain experienced from such people. The indifference, the distance, the disinterestedness, the detachment are hardly missed by working people, and while my illustration is from a sanitized Broadway musical, these responses can be readily found in the research literature, but even more so in the concrete lived lives of working people.

My mind moves quickly to the bourgeois stereotype of sensuous restraint; of suppressed, if not repressed, emotion; of a rationalized (utilitarian) orientation to life—with elitist taste the avowed exception; and workaholics who are uncomfortable unless they are on the job. When I worked in the oil field we used to say that men like these "made love with a washrag in their hand," suggesting that even in the bedroom they had to keep things tidy, neat, and in place, and they could not "let go" even in such basic erotic expression as that of sexual love (though we decidedly would not have said it in the last eleven words I just used).

Working-Class Taste: "Rowdy and Loud at the Twist and Shout"

In contrast to elitist, upper-class taste, that of the working class is quite different. The spectator participates very actively in the event, as I did at the opera. The pleasures are more intense, direct, and immediate.[5] There is great interest in revelry. It involves raucous laughter, plain talk, immediate satisfaction, and physical reaction. The difference can be sharply stated by contrasting two authorities. Listen first to Kant:

> Taste that requires an added element of charm and emotion for its delight, not to speak of adopting this as the measure of its approval, has not yet emerged from barbarism.[6]

But then listen to this country lyric:

> No, we don't fit in with that white collar crowd
> We're a little too rowdy and a little too loud
> But there's no place that I'd rather be than right here
> With my red neck, white socks, and Blue Ribbon Beer.[7]

Working-class taste is indeed "rowdy and loud" and must charm the senses. Perhaps no other artistic form of working-class art more tellingly articulates working-class taste, which is profoundly related, of course, to its popularity among so many working Americans. Hank Williams, Jr. throws a party for all his "rowdy friends," and even Mary Chapin Carpenter, whose work has a crossover quality and a middle-class subjectivity about it, writes music about "Down at the Twist and Shout." Mel Tillis's song "Stay Around a Little Longer" ("Stay all night / stay a little longer / dance all night, dance a little longer"), has the kind of revelry and festivity characteristic of working-class taste that is well represented in country music. Garth Brooks sings about the "American Honky-Tonk Bar Association": "It represents the hardhat / Gunrack, achin'-back / Over-taxed, flag-wavin' fun-lovin' crowd / Their heart is in the music/And they love to play it loud." Meanwhile, Ronnie Dunn is making music so that the folks can do the "Boot-Scootin' Boogie."[8]

Part of the issue here is that working people are more oral than literate. They think in proverbs, stories, and relationships more than in propositions, concepts, and discourse. It is not that they are illiterate, though some are, it is rather that they engage the world in oral terms, rather than the more literate forms of the university trained.[9] They work not so much with ideas about ideas but with ideas about events, to use Robin Horton's helpful distinction.[10] And as Walter Ong has shown, so much of oral thought is oriented around memory, and as such it attempts to make things memorable.[11] For this reason, among other reasons, in a complicated snarl of motivations and concerns, country music must pose itself in heavy formulaic characters, in agonistic struggle, and in festivity that "lets the hellcat roar!"

It also needs to be said that country music as used by working people simply may not be available to people who have not known the working-class world. If one has not worked physically hard; if one has not known dead-end, monotonous, boring jobs; if one has not done such work that must be endured for what happens when one is not working, for which the reward is extrinsic and not intrinsic to the job; if one has not endured an ecology of demeaning "rituals" in a class society; if one has not felt the assault of the psychobabble of the university trained on working people whose lives are far more concrete and situationally formed; if one has not listened to highly differentiated language used to comb the innards of the subjective life of the privileged, when such language seems fluff to people who have work and service occupations under close supervision by bosses who do not "give a damn about what they feel"; if one has not done or does not do such things, then country music as practiced by working people simply is beyond the world of the privileged, and perhaps beyond their reach.

It is important to see country music and working-class taste as a range of practices. Otherwise it is too easy to develop an intellectual appropriation of it that presumes an "empathy" not available except through the practices of working-class life and country music, or that vaunts a dismissive superiority wrought by being "down on" what one is not "up on."

Practices mediate the world to us, and there are things that cannot be known save through the practice of them. Before ever playing a round of golf I remember as an average baseball player saying that "hitting a ball sitting still couldn't be very hard to do." I could only be that far "off base" by talking about something I had never done.

Intellectuals, academics, and elitists have often not been inhibited by their ignorance in talking about working people and their taste. I don't mean only dear old Kant, who defines art—inconsistently—and then determines who is barbaric by his own imperialistic decree. Susanne K. Langer in her *Philosophy in a New Key*, a classic on the philosophy of aesthetics, writes about "the striking indifference of the uneducated masses to artistic values."

In past ages, these masses had no access to great works of art; music and painting and even books were the pleasures of the wealthy; it could be assumed that the poor and vulgar would enjoy art if they could have it. But now, since everybody can read, visit museums, and hear great music at least over the radio, the judgment of the masses on these things has become a reality, and has made it quite obvious that *great art is not a direct sensuous pleasure.*[12]

Susanne Langer received her A.B. degree from Radcliffe, her M.A. from Radcliffe, her Ph.D. from Radcliffe, and taught at Radcliffe, the University of Delaware, New York University, and Columbia University. How could she know what is accessible to anyone outside of the insulated academic world in which she lived?

She makes my point as she continues: "If it [great art] were [a direct sensuous pleasure], it would appeal—like cake or cocktails [To which class do you suppose she belongs?]—to the untutored as well as to the cultured taste."[13] With such sweeping dismissals of the "untutored masses" one would expect Susanne Langer to provide some data, some studies on these "masses." She does discuss anthropology and primal societies, albeit with no little paternalism, and she seems to be versed in the contemporary studies of apes, chimpanzees, and other primates, but I cannot find one reference to anthropological studies about the "untutored masses." My suspicion is that they are of so little mystery to her and so easily "understood" without engagement, that no such serious study is required.

A Dominated Aesthetic

Let's turn from elitist taste to that of the working class. Pierre Bourdieu points out that lower-class taste is a dominated aesthetic; that is, it must continually define and legitimate itself in reference to the dominant elitist taste.[14] You often find country music artists projecting an image of themselves as "ordinary people," as not highfalutin, as just one of the folks. Such framing of themselves defines country artists as clearly not in the elitist group. They are "down home"; they are coal miner's daughters from Butcher Holler, or like Minnie Pearl from Grinder's Switch. They are Wichita linemen or country boys or men who assemble the cars by day and do the bars by night in Detroit City. They are Okies from Muskogee or outlaws or hardworking men who like their whiskey in a fruit jar. They are women in tight jeans, and some of them take their love to town while others stand by their man.

Sometimes this self-definition takes the form of defiance. In "Friends in Low Places" Garth Brooks sings about his unexpected attendance at the formal "black tie affair" of his ex-girlfriend and her new love, at an obviously upper-class setting.

He tells her in the song that she can "blame it" on his "roots," that he "showed up in boots." Admitting that he is not big on proper social graces, he apologizes for ruining the high-class event, but makes it clear that he has "friends in low places," "down at the Oasis," "where the whiskey drowns and the beer chases my blues away." In the videotape of this song, Garth tells the audience that after listening to the words on the radio he decided that he needed another verse because he did not do on the first rendition what he would really do in a situation like that. So he sings a new verse in which he tells his "ex": "That as soon as I finish this glass / Sweet little lady / I'll head back to the farm / And you can kiss my ass!"[15]

Sometimes the music takes a different turn entirely as when there is a coming together of these differences in taste. This usually occurs, as one might guess, through the miraculous power of love. Wayland Holyfield wrote a song called "New York Wine and Tennessee Shine" in which he states "You're silks and satins? / I'm old blue jeans / I'm beat-up trucks / You're Fifth Avenue / I'm country roads/All we got in common / Is that we love each other."[16] Bobby Goldsboro wrote "The Cowgirl and the Dandy," in which Brenda Lee sang "I was Mogen David Wine/He was Chablis '59 / But we sat, the cowgirl and the dandy / He was ski resorts in Aspen / And summers in Paree / I was Grand Ole Opry . . . Nashville, Tennessee." In each of these songs the cultural difference is overcome by the love of the man and woman for each other.[17]

These few examples only touch the surface, of course, but they suggest the extent to which country music is a dominated aesthetic and, further, the degree to which it is self-conscious about the question of taste. This awareness sometimes takes a defensive tone, more often a defiant one, and occasionally pursues a reconciling purpose.

The Taste of Necessity

Bourdieu contends that lower-class taste is the taste of necessity, which "implies a form of adaptation to and consequently acceptance of the necessary, a resignation to the inevitable."[18] He is suggesting the powerful conditioning effect of social life lived under constraint. "The taste of necessity imposes a taste for necessity."[19] In lives where one is either "up against the wall" or constantly aware of how close to the line life can be, it would be pointless to think such an existence would have no effect on a community's framing of things, choices, attitudes, forms of appreciation, standards of judgment, and patterns of perception. Working-class life cannot be appreciated and will not be engaged if these issues are not taken into account.

The taste of necessity takes form in a great variety of ways. For one thing, in a world of constraint, when you get the chance, "you let it all hang out." In doing so, it will be "rowdy and loud," and you "turn it loose." Most working-class jobs are done under close supervision and often in highly coordinated work schedules. That eight-hour day, sometimes with overtime, comes around with great regularity. The pressing demands of hard physical work, often in repetitive monotony, take their toll. The opportunity "to let it go," "to shake loose," "to get down," "to blow it out," "to have a good time," become basic forms of leisure. This emotion plays a profound role in the construction of working-class taste. It would be truly strange if it were otherwise.

To be sure, not all working-class leisure takes this direction. For some the work is numbing, and the time away from work can be an exercise in anesthetic leisure, a circumstance not missed in country music. When Merle Haggard sings "I Think I'll Just Stay Here and Drink,"[20] or when Willie Nelson sings "Whiskey river, take my mind, you're all I got to take care of me,"[21] one begins to see just how much the music is in touch with working life, and how much it represents the range of its practices.

Moreover, not all working-class jobs pay poorly or represent dull, routine work. Some, the minority, pay well. This does not in most cases change the taste. Remembering "where one came from," "not getting above your raisin'," avoiding upper-status practices: all these remain important because pretention to status is the violation of taboos deeply written into working-class life. Additionally, even with affluence and good work, certain practices have formed working people and shaped their feelings, senses, and thought through the profound impact of a world lived without upper-status privilege. After certain practices have formed aesthetic needs and satisfactions, these are not easily set aside. I do know people who, through education and upward mobility, have left their working-class roots and "shut down" these dimensions of their lives. In doing so, many of them repress their aesthetic lives in denial and seek to find expression in alien arts.

Living under constraint has another effect in terms of making it count in matters of taste. This often takes the form of "more flash for the cash" and "cheap substitutes for . . . rare goods."[22] When the money is short, as it is for most working people, the impact on taste will be direct, and country music reflects it. Listen to the lines of a well-known lyric written by Carl Perkins and sung by Elvis: "One for the money, two for the show / Three to get ready, now go cat go / Now don't you step on my blue suede shoes / You can do anything but lay off my blue suede shoes. . . . You can knock me down, step on my face / Slander my name all over the place / Do anything that you want to do / But uh-uh, Honey, lay off of my [blue suede] shoes."[23]

Try not to miss the self-parody in the song. The writer, the singer, and the country music listeners know it is funny and recognize the dynamic of more "flash for the cash." The song is an overstatement, but it is the hyperbole that names something very real in the lives of working people, and they know it. They can laugh about it. The exaggeration of the song helps to get distance on the characteristic and to admit it is there. I happen to love Dolly Parton's music, and no one is better at this kind of self-parody. She often says about her professional dress: "It costs a lot of money to look this tacky." Then why do it? Most anyone in this society who grew up in a working-class world remembers a time when they lived out the fantasy of "more flash for the cash." Naming it, laughing about it, celebrating it in a country music lyric with a pulsing rock beat somehow takes it to another level. It becomes a reclaiming, a warm and hearty "owning," a return to something one does not want to lose, because it points to something too important to let it get away.

I remember in college I had a bright turquoise, corduroy shirt that I liked very much. I also had a pair of turquoise pants, even brighter. To wear them together only augmented the effect and my affect. It was my favorite casual outfit until a dear friend of mine, a young woman, pulled me aside and told me not to wear it.

"Why?"

"Well, it says too much. You need either pants or a shirt that contrasts with the other."

"Why?"

"You just do. You don't wear the same color when the shades are slightly off."

That word "off" did it. I didn't understand it, but I never wore the outfit again. Yet, one of my fantasies is to find a bright turquoise, corduroy shirt and an even brighter pair of pants, and to wear them to my favorite honky-tonk and to do the bop to "Blue Suede Shoes." There are things in life too precious to be repressed.

Third, working-class taste, as a dominated aesthetic, will often be expressed as an inversion of elitist taste. As in the song "Rednecks, White Socks and Blue Ribbon Beer" discussed above, it is clear that rowdy and loud doesn't fit in with a white-collar crowd, presumably more moderated and restrained. Moreover, identity in the music is determined by a sharp distinction between country folks and city people. Or, when the music is about urban workers, the distinction will be made between hardworking men and women and their bosses. For example, Barbara Mandrell "was country when country wasn't cool," or Dolly's characterization of her boss in the song "9 to 5." Even in the songs "The Cowgirl and the Dandy" and "New York Wine and Tennessee Shine," in which the writers attempt to reconcile these tastes, there is no question that the distinction is sharply drawn and well understood.

Finally, working-class taste will tend to fulfill functions. It cannot afford the purposeless purposefulness of Kant's aesthetic. It does need to charm, to provide moral example, to be pleasureful, to be pretty, to be agreeable. In a world of necessity, you can't screw around with abstract aesthetic purity. For example, you don't want an abstract painting for $1,500 that looks like an overused painter's palette, not when you can get a five-foot by four-foot landscape from K-Mart that costs $20 and puts a mountain scene with stream and distant horizon against the wall above the couch. You never saw $1,500 on a paycheck in your life, and the opportunity to own a painting that is a mystery to your friends and to you only reminds you of the high sounding talk of those fancy people you see on public television.

The Politics of Prestige and Distinction

We depict a form of upper-class, elitist taste characterized by an approach to aesthetics and music that seeks "art for art's sake," one that manifests a mood of indifference, detachment, disinterestedness, and distance. In contrast to this elitist aesthetic we spell out a working-class taste that is more rowdy and loud, that celebrates in festivity or moans the hard times, that revels in active participation and physical enjoyment or laments loss and drowns the blues in whiskey and beer, that is plain speaking and expressed in hearty laughter or tears and despair, that will often mock and debase elitist expressions and that lets it "all hang out."

Further, this working-class taste has reason for looking like the opposite of elitist taste. It is a dominated aesthetic and will define itself over against the posturing of elitist sophistication, and thereby as the opposite of highfalutin, fancy ways.

What is going on here? Is there such a thing as aesthetic purity and autonomy of the kind seemingly presumed in elitist taste? Is country music "vulgar," not merely in the sense of being common, but in some more vile, nasty, low-life sense? And why are these distinctions so filled with disgust? Or, is there an underbelly of struggle over the framing of things aesthetic and contest over distinctions following such legitimating definitions of taste and position?

I must confess that when I find cultural distinctions so closely related to class differences, I get suspicious. I am especially so here. How do such loaded feelings and aesthetic claims relate to structured social inequality? How do these cultural definitions operate in the practices of a society and affect its relationships? In short, is there a politics of aesthetics at work here, and what is the role of such a politics in contests over power, privilege, and prestige? We turn to these questions next.

Chapter 2
Elitist Taste and the
Politics of Aesthetics

I still remember as a boy in the third grade joining Miss Ellie Barton's rhythm band, a program designed to teach us Mississippi girls and boys "good music." Miss Ellie had a college degree in music—no small achievement in Mississippi for a woman in the 1940s—and she was an authority. We learned simple rhythms on drums, cymbals, triangles, and sticks, and we often listened to "good music," which was usually from composers like Freml and Romberg. I am sure that Miss Ellie's tastes ran to Bach, Beethoven, Mozart, and Brahms, but she must have looked for something in the light opera of Freml and Romberg to capture the attention of unruly boys like me. I recall liking Romberg's "The Riff Song," with its adventurous, heroic, pulsing equestrian quality, which I often sang bravely as I rode a sweet gum stick horse across my backyard and down the drainage ditch, chasing evil bandits and other enemies of the desert or prairie.[1]

It was in Miss Ellie's class that I learned for the first time that country music was "bad music." I distinctly remember the experience. My mother loved country music and woke me every morning with a kiss on the cheek and with the music playing loud on the radio. I can still feel physically what I felt in being told country music was bad music. On the one hand, I felt a sense of getting taller, because I had learned something that most people in Mississippi must not know since they so absolutely bought into it. On the other hand, it was the first time I can remember my mother being smaller, or not "enough." Back then I had no words for these feelings. I just knew I had not had them before. While I believed I was learning something important, I also felt a strange difference from my mother for the first time.

The Struggle over Distinction

The struggle over music and other forms of art is far more than an aesthetic one. It is permeated with the politics of distinction, with contestation over prestige. It is easy to forget that culture is an arena over which we do battle. Think for a moment about the distinction between high culture and low culture, the refined and the popular, highbrow and lowbrow, the aristocratic and the vulgar, the "pure gaze" and "the naive" one. These distinctions are writ deeply into our cultural psyches and provide rules and frames for the rituals of everyday life that define "who's with it" and "who's not," who's sophisticated and who's banal, and who's got "class" and "who ain't."

It would be years before I realized how much I was swept into these struggles. I don't remember the words my parents used to urge me to do the rhythm band or later to take up the cornet in the fourth grade. Somehow I understood that it was "good for me." I do remember that within a very short time I had begun to feel a sense of the superiority of classical to country music, and by the time I was in the seventh and eighth grades I had a small collection of works by the classical composers.

These were the years when I first became aware of social class. To be sure, it was not a sharply developed awareness. Mainly I noticed the difference in the clothes that kids wore to school, in the different smells of my classmates—especially the ones who did not have indoor plumbing—in the words they used, and the difference it made about the part of town in which you lived. There was also something about the way the teachers treated us. They were fine women, and almost all of them had dedicated their entire lives to teaching. At the same time I knew that the kids from the silk stocking district in my hometown were "different." Their parents were sometimes invited to school to "give talks," and I can remember that I had never heard people talk like that (this was before television). The words they used, the references they made, the kinds of things they talked about were from another world.

Somewhere in all this I learned to defer to such people, and I realized that when I was around them I felt as if I was always "looking up." I can still remember chance meetings in the community when "we" would talk with "them." I could just feel that they were "better" than we were.

At the end of the war my dad had made enough money to buy a small cafe and then, shortly thereafter, to sell it and buy a small taxi cabstand in Brookhaven. We became middle class, which really meant that we inhabited a middle ground. We weren't the hoi polloi or the hoity-toity. As soon as I was old enough to answer the phone and write down addresses, I worked part-time there and would later drive when I turned sixteen.

No place is better to see the underbelly of a small town than a cabstand. People come there from every part of town and in all conditions: Drunks, hustlers, sharks, strangers, the "fine people," and "good folks." You see the rich in compromised circumstances, and the poor in their destitution. You take drunks home who have just that payday spent a week's earnings, and watch their families come out the front door to see if they made it home with anything. You talk to people the night before they commit murder or suicide. You see an upright woman of the community giving away her virtue to two men in the backseat of a cab in a desperate act of passion growing out of some unanswered need that I could not fathom. It is a helluvan education.

Meanwhile I was learning a language of difference. There were the reputable people and the trash, the people from "the good part of town" and from "the wrong side of the tracks," the respectables and the "no goods."

More than this I learned how to participate in the rituals of deference and demeanor that populated the meetings of that community: how to defer to those who were above me and how to sense my own "superiority" with those "below me."

With these I had some kind of awareness, not verbalized, that my demeanor, my bearing shifted from encounter to encounter, as did that of the people I engaged.

I remember two cab trips that occurred within the same hour in those years. In the first a man drunk on rot-gut whiskey showed up at the stand, and I took him home. Few things smell worse than rot-gut whiskey on the breath of a man who has been drunk for a couple of days. At first he wanted to fight me, but by then I had learned what to say to inebriated people who wanted to clean my clock, and I remember not only my growing confidence in my "skills" at handling drunks, but also the disdain I felt, not only for his alcoholism but also for his person.

Within fifteen minutes of dropping him off I went to pick up a man who was arguably the most important man in our community and who had attended a fine university. I can still remember how the atmosphere of the cab changed: my demeanor, my words, my deference to him, his own casual sense of being in control, and his understated valuation of his own importance, which was not so much arrogance as assurance.

With the drunk man I plainly felt that I was "looking down" on him. When the "important man" got in the car, I was "looking up," although I was four or five inches taller than he. More than that, I knew he, too, was an alcoholic and I had transported him in just about the same condition as the previous customer. (The important man about town merely drank better whiskey.) But the intoxicated man was poor, and we called him a "drunk." In contrast, the man of distinction "suffered from an alcohol problem."

E. P. Thompson says that class is not a thing, and it is not a structure.[2] Class happens. It is a prescient comment. Class happens in the clothes people wear, in the things they do and don't do that make them smell differently, in their talk and what they talk about, in the practices that denote "good breeding" and in those that don't, in the kind of whiskey they drink, and how well they can cover their "impaired moments" (we always made sure the man of distinction was not "embarrassed"). Class happens in the everyday encounters—I like to call them rituals—of inequality, where one person commands respect and the other provides it, where one person gives orders and the other takes them, where deference is offered and received and where one's bearing/demeanor shifts to reflect one's place in the schemes of class.

These happenings of class are permeated with matters of taste. As I continued to play my cornet and identified with my teachers, it became increasingly clear that classical music was associated with "education," "refined taste," and "substance." We even said it had "class"; on the one hand, realizing exactly what we meant, and, on the other, as we shall see, utterly oblivious to how radically true such a claim was. In one sense, I had no idea of the degree to which I was an active participant in a struggle for distinction. I swam too much in a sea of inequality to be aware that I was engulfed by it. I think I had no way to distinguish my dignity from the distinction I sought through education and my strivings for upward mobility.

So clear now also is the role of language in supporting the realities of class and in defending the canons of refined taste. It was clear that "cultured taste" was classical music, and country was the music of hillbillies, the riffraff, and honky-tonks. It was trashy music.

Such language supplies the verbal resources for the rituals of supremacy that populate the deference and demeanor of social intercourse. They are the stuff of a pejorative social ecology for people with popular taste who are downscale in the class structure. Such language and the rituals of supremacy constitute strategies of condescension in the politics of taste. They are used for gaining distinction for their perpetrators at the expense of the objects of their ridicule. It is an utterly extraordinary language of difference, a language that excludes others even as it includes its own kind.

Edward Said has said that culture is a system of inclusions and exclusions, suggesting the powerful role of dividing the world into "them and us."[3] No little inclusion and exclusion goes on in elitist taste. I am struck by a rather constant effort to put it out of the reach of most people, to make it unavailable. Primarily, it seems to come from "good breeding and refinement," usually meant in a way not within the reach of most people. Or, for those not coming out of upper-class circumstances, it requires a learned capacity for reflection of a rather abstract sort, a practice usually available to those who have pursued long training in the academy or a school of the arts. Both of these sources of elitist taste do no little distancing, one directly related to the inclusion of the few at the expense of the many. More than that, the distancing itself legitimates the position of the "cultured" against the "vulgar."

Moreover, polar opposites like the cultured and the vulgar are politically loaded. For this reason, it is a good idea to be on guard when groups, especially powerful ones, begin to use binary opposites like these.[4] Such polarities designate differences, and in the politics of class they tend to be polarities of invidious comparison.[5]

A few years back I was looking for a new car and took my pickup as a possible trade-in. The salesperson told me that while I had a means of transportation that was "perhaps practical," I needed a vehicle that would express my "financial maturity" and my "position." Notice how his polar opposite of "perhaps practical" and "financial maturity/position" opened up a line of dialogue that had not even been in my mind prior to then, but which framed our "discourse" about the potential sale.[6]

Moreover, this polar opposite not only defined the situation to his advantage, it also disparaged my love of pickups and placed my "taste" in a "lower" and more extrinsic mode (i.e., practical), not to mention the fact that he had declared me "maturationally delayed" in my vehicular appreciation by continuing to hold to a taste no longer appropriate to my "position." Mind you, he did not consider the beauty of pickups, which I will contend—not on philosophical grounds but on the basis of my heritage—are more beautiful than cars. In protest, I did not buy his dratted car and did not trade my pickup but gave it to my father. Ever since I have been driving the 1990 pickup I bought that week from another agency, and, of course, another salesperson.

Polarities like those of the salesperson are used all the time in the politics of class. They play powerful roles in the struggle over status. Language structures reality, and the binary opposites of language are not only central to linguistic definitions of reality but are deeply involved in both structuring and legitimating social inequality. As such they are powerfully ideological. Moreover the use of these binary opposites in classifying taste as in "high" and "low" culture places aesthetics at the heart of the struggle over distinction and renders it a weapon in dynamics of inclusion and exclusion.

Questioning the "Purity" of High Art and Classical Music

It is clear to me that we need to question sharply the ideology of elitist taste. Fortunately that critique is already underway. In what follows I can only suggest some of the outlines of that work, but it is substantive and very significant.

Paul Dimaggio has shown how the polar opposites of "high art" and "popular art," or the so-called "lesser arts" (sometimes called primitive art, which would include crafts and decorative arts) emerged historically for social rather than aesthetic reasons. Early in the nineteenth century in Boston the arts were a largely undifferentiated mixture of levels, types, and styles. They drew the appreciation and participation of a broad cross section of people from the upper-middle class to the working class. Dimaggio reports that "Museums were modeled on Barnum's" and that "fine art was interspersed among such curiosities as bearded women and mutant animals." By the end of that century, however, sharp divisions had been made between "high" and "low" culture, and these were deeply rooted in class relations.[7]

Because the "higher arts" and "classical music" have been used so often to disparage popular taste and specifically country music, I will examine elitist claims more closely to see if "high culture" is as pure, as autonomous, as transcendent, as absolute, as free of extrinsic matters, as removed from the more sullied aspects of human life as elitist taste maintains. After a look at this we will then be ready to offer an approach to music, including country, that does not necessarily involve

47

such supremacist posturing and yet does not result in an utter relativism.

What is perhaps most important to see in the use of elitist taste is the absence of any basis, any foundation for its universal, objective claims of supremacy. It's hardly ever a bad idea to look carefully at the claims of prestige. These claims have profound tendencies to harbor pretense. This is certainly true of the dominant aesthetic of Western culture, which has held sway now for more than two hundred years. What follows here is a questioning of excessive claims about classical music, especially the claims of autonomy and of absolute music. By doing so it is my hope to raise suspicion about the use of it to legitimate inequality and to bring sharply into view its co-optation in the struggle for distinction.

The Sociohistorical Location of Art

I don't mean to damage the music, as if I could, but I believe that the music is too important to be used by so-called "cosmopolitans" to advance their prestige or by the upper class to brace its privilege. This, of course, does not mean the music is above criticism. Vulnerability to criticism is simply a condition of being human. No one and nothing constructed by humans gets everything right or leaps out of and transcends the limitations of its own time and place, its worldview, its captivity to cultural formations and to concrete lived existence. This leads to my first point, which is that all art—and certainly music—is socioculturally and historically located. In the space we have here I can deal with basically two aspects of this much larger issue.[8]

The first of these is "the autonomy of the arts." This is virtually synonymous with Kant's idea of pure taste and "art for art's sake." The work of Janet Wolff demonstrates the profound impact of sociocultural and historical influences on the arts. They are social products and emerge out of time and place and cannot under such examination be regarded as "autonomous." She names a number of factors that influence the arts and calls for deeper investigation of these. Among the factors needing attention are: (1) patronage, (2) the production and distribution of major art institutions, (3) the role of the state in cultural production, (4) the race/class/gender of cultural producers, (5) the characteristics of the consumers of art (i.e., audience), and (6) technological resources such as print, reproduction capacities, and so on.[9]

The second of these, absolute music, is sometimes seen as the exception to arts that are socially and historically conditioned because, in this view, it is understood to represent nothing but music itself. Carl Dahlhaus, for example, defines this view of "absolute music" as "independent instrumental music," which "purely and clearly expresses the true nature of music by its very lack of concept, object, and purpose." It is seen as "pure structure," representing itself. It is "detached from the affections and feelings of the real world, it forms a separate 'world for itself.'"[10]

Dahlhaus, however, after tracing the development of "absolute music" through the twists and turns of its history states that "the idea of 'pure musical matter' is an illusion based on a violent abstraction from the historical and social character of music." He points out that the very idea of "pure musical matter," is "based on a set of preconditions in the history of ideas."[11] Such music is hardly "autonomous" or "absolute."

The Semiotic Study of Music

In her discussion of the sociocultural and historical influences on music, Janet Wolff also calls for a semiotic analysis. Semiotics is the study of signs used in the coding of a culture.[12] In this sense Wolff is calling for study of the signs used in music and for a decoding of them to discover how they are socially used.

The work of Susan McClary is a good example of such semiotic analysis. She focuses, for example, on the social construction of conventional signs in classical music to denote gender and the ways these signs function to define men and women. She is, of course, interested in the means by which these codes are used ideologically to serve the interests of men. Her work suggests profoundly sexist ingredients in opera and other classical music. Such ingredients call severely into question notions of musical purity.[13]

The Arts, Music and Class

The use of the arts, of course, figures heavily in issues of class. Lawrence Levine's work on the rise of cultural hierarchy in the United States demonstrates how cultural categories are invented in order to make social inequalities appear "natural" and thereby deny the creative and artistic endeavors of an entire social class in wholesale fashion. Levine calls attention to the racist use of the very terms "highbrow" and "lowbrow." These terms emerge from the pseudoscience of phrenology in which its nineteenth-century practitioners associate moral character and intellectual ability with certain types of brain size and cranial shape. In constructing this hierarchy these "scientists" put themselves, of course, in the superior or "highbrow" category. As categories of "highbrow," "middlebrow," and "lowbrow" come into general usage, these are hardly neutral terms but suggest the relative value of certain groups and the quality of their creative and artistic work. Social class is especially coded with this hierarchy and the working class and certain nonwhite races are accorded primitive status.[14]

Robert Walser points out that this kind of racism and classism are still at work in our own time. "People are constantly being typed by their cultural allegiances, respected or dismissed because of the music they like." What is worse is that people then internalize these things and believe them about themselves and about the creative capacities of their own traditions. Walser concludes that "cultural hierarchy functions to naturalize social hierarchies through the circular reinscription of prestige."[15]

To sort through the arts and music in the light of such studies of the role of gender, race, and class in classical or in any music is to see with new eyes the facades of "autonomy" and of "art for art's sake." It is not necessary to reject completely the forms and genres of art so conditioned by their social locations, but it is time to stop the ludicrous claims about their purity when they are deeply implicated in the legitimation of social inequality.

An emerging body of analysis and evidence of this sort increasingly characterizes the field of musicology. The sociohistorical influences on the arts and on music seem clear. That music, even "absolute music," is reflective of the structure of social inequality and indeed implicated in it cannot be denied. These issues need to be faced. We are not served by fictions of "purity" and "autonomy."

In the Absence of Known Foundations

In the light of this kind of social and historical conditioning, sharp questions must be raised about any music as somehow transcendent, universal, and timeless. While doubtlessly some classical music will continue to play an important role throughout the world for the foreseeable future, claims of universality and timelessness surely are vaulted, and, even if some of this music should last yet centuries more, how would one know it was universal, how would one know it was timeless?

Such claims may have expressive value to shout one's appreciation and love of the music, as lovers so often do about each other, but certainly such claims dare not to be taken as music for all times and places and throughout all cultures, world without end.

Yet, one might answer that indeed the claims of universality and timelessness can be established other than through an empirical waiting out of the centuries, that indeed elitist taste and classical music have some defense in a foundation of aesthetic excellence that establishes their claims without an empirical universality and timelessness (whatever in the world those might actually be).

But it is a commonplace of contemporary philosophy that such foundations cannot be established or, at least, we do not know how to establish them, a topic we shall turn to in a later chapter. The burden of proof seems to be clearly on those who would make such foundationalist claims.

Critical Judgment in a World Without Foundations

Not all of the specific tastes of any genre or people are to be highly evaluated, or, for that matter, are to be simply reduced to their sociocultural, historical conditioning. Evaluation is basic to the discriminate judgment of any practice of the arts. For example, there are criticisms to be made of country music, and a blanket endorsement of country music as an unbroken history of good music or of a cultural supremacy of its own would be foolish indeed. Below, I will propose an approach to the aesthetics of music that will take seriously an understanding of various styles of music as traditions formed in publics through their practices of composition, performance, enjoyment, and so on. These publics and their traditions develop standards of perception, judgment, and appreciation, by which a music is to be evaluated.

Criticism is central to the practice of any art. But there is a great deal of difference between critique within a tradition by those who have apprenticed themselves as its practitioners, on the one hand, and the ideological use of binary opposites of language in rituals of supremacy that advance an authoritarian politics of taste, on the other.

The invidious comparisons between traditions of music in the wider culture and especially between the classes is far more accurately understood as a struggle over prestige and status. Art is a battleground for cultural superiority, and the stature that flows from it. When one thinks of the feelings of disgust generated in people by their aversion to country music, especially when they often know little about it and—in the case of most advocates of, say, classical music, who cannot really establish in terms of some philosophical ground a defensible case for its superiority—one can appropriately suspect that cultural rivalry is going on. At this point we are into the politics of distinction.

The Role of Aesthetics in the Legitimation of Inequality

It is interesting, indeed, that the very people who so often defend the sophistication and purity of the arts are the very people who are the most naive and the most egoistically served by their views. (Indeed, if they are not naive, then even more serious moral dereliction is afoot.) My point is that aesthetics participates actively in the legitimation of inequality.

One should not miss the vocabularies of supremacy and the binary opposites of ideology at work in elitist taste. Note that classical music is seen as good music, and country is seen as simplistic, commercial, and lacking in depth. A whole range of such polarities is at work in the structuring of the captivities of class: highbrow/lowbrow, sophisticated/naive, cultured/primitive, and refined/common. Such language frames the situation to the advantage of elites and characterizes the lower classes as vulgar.

Jimmy Hope

There is perhaps no better way to see these things than to be a spectator at the deconstruction of a ritual of elitist taste. I have a friend whom I will call Jimmy Hope Smith, who is a Southern Baptist and looks like a stereotyped fundamentalist preacher. Slightly pudgy, he wears his hair in a modified pompadour and, so help me, puts oil on it. When he dresses up, he wears those neon blazers with ties that look like technicolor regurgitation. (Yes, I have tastes of my own; I just don't argue that they are philosophically defensible or universal.)

Jimmy Hope talks in a thick Southern accent sprinkled with a studied use of incorrect English and intentional malapropisms. He also holds a Ph.D. in theology from a major eastern university, and he is one sharp cookie. Philosophically, he has had an ongoing interest in the aesthetics of Kant, Schopenhauer, Santayana, Langer, and Wittgenstein. I have been present at a party when some elitist know-nothing begins to wax elongatedly about the lowbrow tastes of the American people. While Jimmy Hope is quite capable of criticizing this society, elitism of this sort drives him to distraction. He will usually begin by asking the person to define "good taste," and then to explain such taste and how the person would establish it philosophically. If the person happens to know one school of thought, say Kant, Jimmy Hope raises questions from the point of view of one of the other philosophers, introducing no little confusion. Knowing full well that most colleges and universities do not critically establish the tastes they socialize into their students, Jimmy Hope pushes the argument until his prey can simply no longer respond. When a ritual of supremacy turns into a display of ignorance and empty arrogance, the bewilderment that occurs has an earth-shaking quality to it. The ground moves. Suddenly one's location is no longer assured, and the presumed distinction that goes with it is now up for grabs.

Every time I see Jimmy Hope in action, I wish my mother could be there.

PART II

Music as Traditions

Chapter 3
Foundations, Turtles, and Music as Traditions

t Millsaps College I ran into philosophy for the first time. When I went there, I thought courses in that subject were basically instruction in wise sayings and stories that told you how to live. I was dead wrong. I shall never forget the encounter I first had when the fine professors there began to push me on what I really knew I could prove philosophically. I discovered that I could prove nothing! I remember the "comfort" I found when I first ran into Descartes. He had decided to doubt everything. Yet, he argued that when he doubted everything, he could not doubt that there was a doubter. For me this was salvation. At last I had a foundation for my thinking that I could build on.

At the time I was running from everything I had associated with the ministry as I had known it. I was determined not to be "a Bible thumper," "a hellfire and brimstone preacher," who "believed everything in the Bible just like God dictated it." I wanted a faith that could be based in reason and experience, an intellectual appropriation of the "truths" of Christianity but one open to truth wherever I found it.

Somehow in all that inner conflict, I "knew" that Descartes and his doubter and classical music and the "informed ministry" I sought all went together. While I had never made all those connections in thought, I had a conviction that it could be done. I was in rapid flight from the life I had known. I now believe that I was trying to leap out of my cultural skin. I don't mean I needed to be a fundamentalist preacher or an uncritical thinker, and certainly not one who simply took wholesale a good deal of the life I knew from my roots. I mean that I was trying to jump completely out of a tradition—in effect become homeless—in the search for an entirely different world. To be sure, I needed to be alienated from my racism and sexism among other things, but I was also rejecting the working-class world I knew.

Country music, of course, was thoroughly rejected along with the rest. I did not understand it then, but country music simply embodied too much of the working-class life I wanted to leave. When you turn away from the core realities of your soul, you reject its music as well. I don't mean it was wrong to love classical music, which I do with a passion. I don't mean it was a mistake to pursue education and to search for some understanding about the world and its magnificent mystery. Rather, it was the self-surgery in which I engaged, my attempt to amputate the tradition that bore me that was wrong. As faulted as it was, it also had a profound richness about it that I could have claimed even as I raised Cain about its violations.

This was before I "met" Wittgenstein, that strange and wonderful Austrian philosopher, who lived such a tortured life in the first half of this century. He stated that if Descartes had doubted everything, he could not doubt anything at all. Wittgenstein saw, as clearly as anyone, that life is not based in certainty, but in trust, really in trusting activity. It would become a way that I could reclaim my culture and country music, and a new appreciation for the richness of faith that sustained me. His views became a way for me to understand my life and a way to come to terms with country music.[1]

Foundations and Trust

Clifford Geertz tells a wonderful story that comes out of India. An Englishman was told by an Indian that the world rested on a platform, which rested on the back of an elephant, which then rested on the back of a turtle. When the Indian was then asked what this turtle rested on, he replied "another turtle." "And that turtle?" "Another turtle." "And that turtle?" "Ah, Sahib, after that it is turtles all the way down."[2]

It is a very Wittgensteinian thing to say. When attempting to provide a foundation for our most basic beliefs, we seem inevitably to get to a place where there are turtles all the way down. It is a commonplace of contemporary philosophy that there is no known foundation for human knowing in any universal account of experience or in any first principles of reason. We come to a point where we assume the presence of a foundation that cannot itself be established, that is, we arrive finally at a base of trust, not of knowing.

Where does this leave us? With an utter relativism? No, but it does mean our experience and reason are dependent on the traditions in which we live and from which we come. As we shall see, this has important consequences for music and the ways we assess it. Such a view does not require us to be uncritical of our traditions, but rather to see these traditions as ongoing embodied arguments.

Human Life and Thought Reside in Traditions

We are born into communities, into human traditions. We are formed by them. One does not live without them. It is popular in some quarters today to be antitraditional, but one can only argue such a view if one is utterly unaware that such a stance is itself a modernist tradition, and I might add, a very anemic one. No one lives, thinks, feels, knows, oughts, wants apart from a tradition. We do not select them so much as we live in them and through them. As Stanley Hauerwas likes to ask: "Whose story is operating through you?"

No one builds a position in human thought and activity that is not historically and culturally located. Alisdair MacIntyre points out that "there is no set of independent standards of rational justification to adjudicate contending traditions." That is, no one stands on some objective ground where they can assess things in neutrality. All of us operate in a tradition of some kind. While, indeed, what happens in one tradition can be overheard in another, and while traditions can share certain standards, nevertheless each tradition has its own precedents, standards, and background beliefs.[3] This poses the problem then of how different traditions can be compared. When standards vary this greatly, the traditions may not be commensurable and therefore not fully comparable. This has quite direct implications for music as we shall see.

Therefore, I suggest three things. First, the founding of our lives resides in trust and not in knowing. At the base of our thought and other activity are assumptions we cannot prove and cannot establish. With us all, it seems, there comes a point where it is "turtles all the way down."

Second, we are not able, at least so far as we know, to substantiate our views in terms of first principles of reason or some universal account of experience. In the absence of such foundations we do not so much build our views on foundations as we develop "foundations" to support our views.

Finally, our knowing and our other practices do not rest on foundations but reside in traditions. It is from these that we derive our standards of reason, the character of our experience, and the criteria of our knowing.

These learnings brought me to a new way of approaching my own culture and country music.

Music as Traditions

A genre of music is a tradition. There is no foundation by which it can be established; claims of legitimation for a style of music reside finally in some trust; and its skills, excellencies, and standards are developed in the practices of the tradition. There is no way, at least as far as we know now, to "found" art or music by reference to some universal rationality, or some universal account of experience or desire, or satisfaction, or intuition, or emotional expression, or mystical truth, or some nonconceptual form. Such claims reside in some trust not itself established. To rephrase part of MacIntyre's statement above, "there is no standing ground, no place" for the work of musical composition, performance, the development of a discerning and appreciative public, the honing of skills and practices, the forming of discriminate judgment, and the advancement of a music "apart from that which is provided by some particular tradition or other."[4]

Does this mean that music is utterly relative? No, but it does mean it is relative to a tradition. It is socially embodied in a public or publics, it is advanced in practices distinctive to it, it serves goods, and its standards are derived from the work of its practitioners. Let's look more closely at this series of claims.

Country Music as a Tradition

First, country music as a tradition has been socially embodied in the rural and urban working people of the United States throughout the last eight decades of the twentieth century. While its roots go back much further than this, nevertheless our focus is here. It is, to be sure, a commercial music, but I will argue that the music cannot simply be reduced to a reflection of commercial dynamics but must take into account how the music is used by working people, a concern that will now increasingly take focus in this chapter and those to come. It has also attempted to reach out to other groups across its history; this is especially seen in its crossover efforts. The Nashville Sound or countrypolitan and contemporary country are examples. These crossover pursuits on the part of the entrepreneurs, producers, and artists of the music are especially strong at the present time. Still, its primary audience across the years is people who work.

Second, artistic work, like music, comes from the practice of that art. Through the practices of the tradition skills are developed and extended, standards of what constitutes excellence are socially constructed, and tastes become "cultivated," meaning that we come to know what is good in the tradition and what is not according to criteria established in that tradition. A complex form of taste emerges in such an artistic tradition. For example, the formative influences of singers like Jimmie Rodgers and Hank Williams and their impact on later artists like George Jones and even later Dwight Yoakam are a rich part of the tradition. Further, the major directions given the music by Kitty Wells, Patsy Cline, and Loretta Lynn have an abiding influence on the development of the music.

Frank Burch Brown in a helpful discussion argues that taste has three basic elements. Brown maintains that each of these elements "is at once a part of some more encompassing form of taste and also in itself a particular form of taste." The three are: apperception, appraisal, and appreciation.[5]

The first, apperception, is an intellectual process of bringing impressions to awareness and forming them into a coherent imaginative and intellectual order. It is a way to pay attention to and to take in the aesthetic features of art. It is, for example, an informed and trained way of listening and "taking in" music. As such it involves "thought" (often), sensation, and imagination. The input of the senses is necessary but not sufficient for the apperception of taste.[6]

Appraisal, the second, is a "self-consciously critical and evaluative aspect of taste by which one seeks to ascertain the aesthetic excellence of a work or object." It involves "a conscious judgment of aesthetic status." It is taste as discriminating judgment, the capacity to evaluate an artwork whether one personally "likes" it or not.[7]

The third is appreciation, which he defines as having to do with one's personal response and evaluation, that is, whether one "likes" or "dislikes" it. Appreciation involves some kind of appraisal and apperception although Brown maintains that "we can in reflection separate purely personal response from both apperception and considered appraisal."[8]

These kinds of literate, theoretical distinctions are not characteristic of most of the writing and talk about country music. This is so for at least two reasons. For one, there has been so much prejudice against popular culture, and especially country music for so much of its history, that academics and others with theoretical interests basically left it alone. For another, many of the composers and performers come out of backgrounds of rural and working America where intellectual and literate practices of this kind are simply not a part of their world. These folk have been more oral than literate, by which I mean not illiterate, at least in most cases, but rather people who engage the world in oral practices such as thinking in proverbs more than propositional claims and in stories more than in conceptualization and theory.[9]

But it would be an error born of ignorance and probably of bigotry to believe that practices of informed perception, discriminating judgment and learned appreciation do not occur in the music, and these on a complex and expanding scale. Several things need to be brought to mind. First, in each of Brown's dimensions of taste clearly socialization, preparation, training, and the formation of a critical sensibility are required. In a society where so much value is placed on formal preparation, especially in the schooled sense, it is easy to forget the amount of training country artists go through in their work and the critical capacities they develop. Moreover, their training is often done with little "protection" from their audiences. The apprenticeship of nightly and weekend stands, the years they spend in learning the skills and the art, and working in the presence of crowds who know when music is "country" and when it is not can be highly demanding.

For another, the music requires a broad range of skills and competencies. I think particularly of the ability of the music to tell a compelling story. The narrative character of country music is a distinctive dimension of its tradition and one highly developed, especially as seen in the work of someone like Tom T. Hall. McLaurin and Peterson compare country with blues and soul lyrics, rap music, jazz, and bluegrass but argue that it "is unique among the major kinds of contemporary music in telling stories."[10] John Hartford calls them "word movies."[11]

It would be difficult to exaggerate the importance of the storytelling character of country music. Given the oral character of so much of working-class engagement with the world, the narrative makeup of country songs not only tells their stories, but also does so in the most basic indigenous style. More than that, there may be no two things more powerful in human communication than storytelling and music. To put them together in one art form is perhaps as close as one can come to embodying the life of a people.

Furthermore, it has spawned a large number of truly fine

musicians, some of the best in the world in stringed instruments, percussion, and voice. With these the music has made significant innovations in performance, in rhythmic formulations, in the generation of stylistic sounds, and in the development of a semiotic (sign) structure for displaying working-class life in a broad range of its expressions. For example, note the solo guitar work in Jeannie C. Riley's rendition of "Harper Valley P.T.A." It is the story about a young woman accused of not being a fit mother for her daughter because she wears her dresses too short and hangs out in honky-tonks. This mother goes to the next meeting of the P.T.A. and reveals one by one the far more serious hypocrisies of the members of the school board and names names! As the song says, she "socked it to the Harper Valley P.T.A." The guitar solo lays out with artistic clarity not only the cardboard facade of such hypocritical pretense, but as it moves down the scale it captures the collapse of such arrogant moralism under the devastation of the young mother's prophetic fire. It is an artful piece of work.[12]

Yet another development and contrary to what those outside the tradition and untrained to hear it may think, the enormously rich unfolding and refinement of nasal singing is a skill of the first order, one that is truly rare when done well and quite simply electric in its expressive capability and in the power with which it can touch an audience within the tradition. The work of Kitty Wells, Loretta Lynn, Tammy Wynette, Dottie West, and the new, young artist Shania Twain represents a variation on this vocal style among women. Hank Williams, Floyd Tillman, George Jones, Willie Nelson, and Randy Travis maintain this tradition among men.

I will not go into the sophistication of its technicians in sound, reproduction, and visualization, since this is beyond my focus, but they may be among the very best in the world. Much more could be said, but for now this will suggest something of the practices and skills that increasingly make it a rich tradition.

I am hesitant to write about how much bad material there is in country music, because too many people believe it is altogether that. My taste for the music should not be construed as uncritical. I once heard Will Campbell say that "country music is a lot like classical music, most of it is a bunch of junk." He's right. In composition, for example, Music Row hacks abound and anyone who listens to country on the radio knows the mindlessness of many announcers and how dreary the musical selections can be. (But have you listened to the pretentious, serious, officious, smooth-voiced disk jockeys on the classical music stations? They sound like funeral home directors. And does anyone really want to make the case for all this as "good music"?)

On the issue of commercialization, both classical and country have serious problems: listening to a country song while someone tries to sell you picante sauce is a corrupt experience, but have you bought underwear lately at an aspiring department store to the exalted sound of Mozart?

Third, music as a tradition will serve goods. That is, it will in its practices of composition, performance, and enjoyment—among others—serve certain aims. As the tradition develops, it will be judged in its quality by how well it manifests and intrinsically bears in itself the goods the music is meant to serve. For example, as we shall see below, one of the goods of country music is its embodiment of the lived existence of working people. It "sings their lives." To quote Loretta Lynn, it "doesn't beat around the bush," but "tells it like it is."[13] A country music song, then, will be judged, in part, by how well it intrinsically fulfills this goal, this good, this aim. Some of the most bitter conflicts in country music result when breeches of these standards occur. I think especially of the 1970s and the rejection of the Nashville Sound by the "outlaws" and of the expression of disdain in a song like "Are You Sure Hank Done It This Way?"[14] Many of these goods and standards are not formally articulated in theory, conceptualization, and discourse yet, but this is due to the youthfulness of country—less than a century old, its mainly oral working-class public, and the disdain "popular culture" and country music suffer, in the main, from academic and broader artistic circles.[15]

Fourth, a tradition of any complexity will be diverse within itself. This is certainly true of country music. The traditional respectable music of home, family, and faith that received expression in the A. P. Carter family in the twenties is quite different than the "ramblin' man" music of Jimmie Rodgers in that same decade. The honky-tonk music of the late thirties and forties is quite distinct from the forms before it. The Southwestern music of Bob Wills and others took the music in yet another direction, while making permanent contributions to the larger tradition. A diversity can also be found as one moves from the "cowboy sweetheart" music of Patsy Montana, to the "stand by your man" work of Tammy Wynette, to the tough independence of Loretta Lynn, when she tells her man not to "come home a'drinkin' with lovin' on your mind" and what she is going to do now that she's "got the [birth control] pill." The outlaw music, as we saw, took on the Nashville Sound, and the new traditionalists in the nineties protested contemporary country. In this sense the music is an "embodied argument" to use Alasdair MacIntyre's term in struggles over the goods that it serves and the shape of its continuity over time.[16]

Beauty

But what about "beauty"? Where does this leave us on this important question? My contention is that no aesthetic "essence" exists. For example, beauty is not a universal; it is not an ever more highly abstract generality seeking ever more stratospheric definition in some vain hope of a "no thing" characteristic that will cover any such careful definition of it. Such work is really a finessing of language in an attempt to find a phrase that is sufficiently abstract to use in any place that can be so named. Such attempts grow from what Wittgenstein called "the craving for generality."[17]

Beauty, rather, is particular—not in some essential sense—but in its profound characterization of some thing, some event, someone, some moment. The beauty of a long drive in golf, one that begins in a low climbing arc that then achieves length and height in some reaching flight that falls and rolls three hundred yards from the tee, renewing hope as it rests a mere eighty yards from the green. Beauty is the crushing emotional realism of Hank Williams singing "I'm So Lonesome I Could Cry." Beauty is Rodolfo and Mimi erupting in the rapturous words of

"Amor!" "Amor!" and "Ah!" Beauty is the Pietà defying all of nature and all common sense by making the very stones cry out in pathos and grief. Beauty is the smile of the one you love when a whole day or a long week has gone bad and dear friends have let you down. Beauty is the completion of a long day of hard work that drew everything from you, that made you work when you wanted to cry, that called something from you that you didn't know was there. Suddenly there's an emotional, spiritual, physical, mental, tired rush of aesthetic satisfaction that chills you in the completion of the job. Then the project stands like some crystallization of the sweat, and the hardness of the work now becomes intrinsic to the completed aim.

Beauty is intrinsic, but in a distinct sense. There is no one aesthetic end it fulfills. It is not purposeless purposefulness. Rather, beauty is the artistic fulfillment of the aims of a specific genre of art or an event or a moment. That is, every music, every art has aims, but they are all different so far as I can tell. Beauty is the artistic fulfillment of these distinct aims. When Hank Williams sings of loneliness in such a way that he embodies loneliness in the specific practices of country music, that is art, that is beauty. It is that specific, that particular. It is not an essence, but an artistic completion of the particular aims of a given human art and craft.

One may ask whether "artistic" as used in "artistic fulfillment" is not some essence. No, because what is "artistic" is determined by the practices of a tradition, by the skills and excellencies of that embodied articulation of craft, performance, and appreciation, by what is required for the aim to be met well and beautifully. It is not abstract art for art's sake, but the intrinsic expression of the aims of a tradition in the practices of that tradition. This is the intrinsic character of art. If you look carefully at the things beautiful in the wide range I list above, you will find that every one of them is radically different from the others and that each one is a distinct form of beauty: from the golf drive to operatic singing, to Hank Williams's portrayal of loneliness in a song, to the expressions of affection of a loved one, to the aesthetic satisfactions of hard physical work, and so on. The beauty is in the intrinsic fulfillment of the aims of each of these practices.

All of this is to say that Wittgenstein opened a new door for me. He and MacIntyre taught me the importance of trust and tradition in thought and the way to claim one's tradition. Moreover, I came to see music, too, as a tradition, and country music as the embodiment of the working-class tradition out of which I came. My rejection of the music was in great part a result of my rejection of the world from which I came and that rejection was as sharp as it was because the music so powerfully embodied the life from which I turned away. To rediscover the music, to reclaim it as an incarnate testimony of the people from whom you come, to recognize it as a worthy tradition, as a soul music, is an exercise not only in self-discovery but also in cultural restitution.

Over the course of this century, the music developed a vast array of practices and diverse forms within itself. With these have come the formation of skills and standards of excellence and a complex and creative artistic tradition. The music serves a variety of goods and its most important work can be found in the practices and music that are intrinsic to these aims. I turn now to these.

Chapter 4
You Wrote My Life:
The Goods of Country Music

When I rejected country music, there was one sense in which I knew exactly what I was doing. Perhaps not so much in some verbalized, self-conscious form, but I clearly made a choice. It was to put distance between me and the world and the people I came from. Somehow I saw clearly that the music *was* "those people." I did not simply decide I did not "like" country music. It is certainly not necessary that one like any form of music. But I was not making a mere musical choice. I wanted out of that world.

When I left Mississippi in 1957 and went to Boston, in effect I went behind the moon as far as country music was concerned. As long as I was in Mississippi, country music was unavoidable. It was in the air. In Boston I could escape it. While there, my great teachers Walter Muelder, Paul Deats, and Alan Knight Chalmers would never let me forget the issues of working-class people and of social class, but from the time I went to Boston until the demonstration against George Wallace in 1968, I lost contact with the music. While there I even pastored a church of working people for six years, and I was concerned about their "justice issues," but I was out of touch with their lifestyle commitments.

My rejection of the music somehow reflects how clearly that music embodied the lives of the world from which I ran. Country music was then and is now a "music in use."[1] It is a music at work. It is embedded in the lives of working people and serves goods basic to them. In some sense I saw this and turned away from it.

As a music participates in a story, embodies a people, establishes an artistic tradition, communicates a story, develops the excellence and skills of its practices, and sings the people's existence, it is soul. In the case of country music, it gives musical and lyrical statement to the lives of working people, dramatizes and intensifies their experience, provides expressive moment to their feelings, offers itself in working-class taste, celebrates the contradictions of the working world and "sticks it to" a dominate order with indigenous forms of resistance. These are the characteristics that make it white soul. These were the things I rejected.

In my attempt to reclaim the music here I make no argument for an uncritical approach to the music. It, too, participates in inequalities and other systemic injustices. These must not be ignored. Country music is historically located. It is not "pure." But neither is any other kind of music or any other kind of life.

The Aims of White Soul

Country music serves desperately important aims in the lives of working people. Indeed, its aesthetic is based in its capacity to give artistic expression to these aims. Its delight is in the articulation of such aims, its ability to catch the listener in a surprise recognition of self and life in the lyrics of the music. I want to name four such aims or goods, though I hasten to say that such a few by no means exhaust the offerings of the music.

Embodying Working-Class Life

The first of these, and there is a sense in which it overarches the others, is the aim of embodying working-class life. No less an authority than Merle Haggard says "no one could really know [country music] unless they've been there." Charles F. Gritzner paraphrases Haggard with the folk line: "If you ain't lived it, you can't appreciate it."[2]

Reflecting his rural roots, Hank Williams puts it graphically: "You got to have smelt a lot of mule manure before you can sing like a hillbilly. The people who has been raised something like the hillbilly has knows what he is singing about and appreciates it."[3]

Dorothy Horstman reports that it reflects "the religious and moral values of its audience" with "few high abstractions." It has "a reverence for tradition," it is "simple and direct," and "tells it like it is."[4] Tom T. Hall describes it as "workin' for a livin', thinkin' your own thoughts, lovin' your town," but above all "country is all in your mind."[5]

One of the most insightful comments comes from Dolly Parton. She not only speaks to the aim of embodying the lives of the fans, but she also says something to my earlier contention that the people use the music in their own ways. Dolly points out that "The people [who come to country concerts] don't come to see you be you, but *to see you be them*, and what they want to be."[6]

"To see you be them" and "what they want to be" addresses deep recesses of what country music is about. Many observers note the place of sincerity and authenticity in country performers, and the necessity of them being "one of us." The point is that the artists attempt to embody the people in their own performances.

In this connection we see the role of self-parody among performers for keeping this relationship in place. In 1994, Reba McEntire wore a very low-cut gown to the Academy of Country Music Awards show. Her attire triggered no little debate among country fans about its appropriateness. Sandi Spika, Reba's hair and wardrobe designer for seven years, thought it was "revealing in a classy way." But the gown caused such a reaction during the show that Reba remarked on stage: "I wish Sandi would have told me I had that [gown] on backwards."[7]

There are plenty of women, and men, in the working world who are not a little insecure about style. To have a country show queen of Reba's stature make fun of herself touches something very serious and displays a genuine predicament that few of the fans have not known. You do not live in a world in which the dominant etiquette is not your own without having endured scalding social blunders. When Reba can make fun of herself and trigger in the minds of her listeners their own stories about times when they did something inappropriate and embarrassing, they feel a kinship with her. She really is "like us."

They also hear the humor. They know that Reba knows which side of the dress is the front, but by parodying herself she is getting out of a crunch in terms of the negative reaction. They, too, have "screwed up," even when they thought they knew what they were doing. To wear or say something you really think is "with it" and then to discover "it ain't right," simply comes with the territory of living in an alien etiquette. To watch her sidestep the blunder without pulling rank, to watch her keep her cool, to see her "own up" to a "lack of sophistication," by making her social "know-how" about such things seem even less than it actually is, to see her face up to a circumstance that could be demeaning, to see her turn embarrassment into humor—all of these remind them of situations in their own lives. They see "one of us" rise to the occasion, and they participate vicariously in her triumph.

To Make the Ordinary Important

The second aim or good of white soul, and closely related to that of embodying the lives of working people, is making the ordinary important. Richard Hoggart characterizes working-class taste and interest in popular culture as "an overriding interest in the close detail" of ordinary, everyday living. Its interest is in what is already known. It does not tell you what you don't know so much as what you do, but it does that in a significant way. Hoggart describes the working-class taste as one that "shows" more than it "explores." The concern is not so much to analyze as to display, not so much to delve into the intricacies of discursive thought and subjective feelings, as to give graphic testimony to the necessities, the tribulations, the joys, the struggles, and the ecstasies of concrete lived life. It attempts not so much to run away from the live-a-day world as to intensify it and make it important, because "ordinary life is interesting."[8]

It needs to be remembered that for the working class, life is rendered unimportant in the work-a-day world. They lose out in the battle for distinction and the prestige rewards of a winner society. The disdain, the discounting, and the arctic dismissals of them and their lifestyles are not lost on them. In addition, the work itself is often hard and boring, and they themselves often feel that "anybody could do my job." But it is a job, they have to have it, they have to do it, things are not likely to change, and they will have this job or one like it for a long time. The best you can do in most situations is to "get used to it." Yet, putting it in words does not give the practices of such lives their due. "Saying it" doesn't get to it. "Living it" is a far deeper reality than discourse about it.

Still, the music does something desperately important in this situation. Most country songs are more "general" than the concrete experience of working people, but these songs invoke significance around the particularities of their lives. When you hear a country artist of no little renown sing lyrics from jukeboxes, radios, and television sets all over the land, and when these songs speak generally to specifics you practice every day, then the ordinary becomes extraordinary, it takes on profound meaning and importance. Your own day-to-day life is implicated in the music: the pain and the pleasure, the wins and the losses, the blues and the celebrations, the boredom and the excitement, the hope and the despair, life and death.

Though country music speaks generally to particularities, this is not exactly true. Country music is typically so tangible and so specific in itself—in its concrete, vital character—that people identify with it and bring their own lives to it.

When a country boy is venerated in a world of city slickers, when a woman is "a sparrow when she's broken," but "an eagle when she flies," when you're a hardworking man who does his "drinking from a Dixie cup" or a woman working "nine to five," when you're "so lonesome you could cry" or so in love that you could "waltz across Texas" with your beloved, when there's "too much month at the end of the money" or you'd "rather have a bottle in front of you than a frontal lobotomy," when you've got "the lovesick blues" or you are in ecstasy about "what goes on behind closed doors," when you want to tell your boss to "take this job and shove it" or you need a friend to help you "make it through the night," then, by God, it is your music and they are singing your song! And what's more, your life, too, is important. It means something. It takes on significance.[9]

Dramatizing and Intensifying Feeling

Such music also dramatizes and intensifies feeling. Often one hears that country is heart music. It sings feelings. The importance of this to the listeners is not lost on the artists. Webb Pierce—who "seemed the very embodiment of the honky-tonk sound," according to Bill Malone—says about hit songs:

> One of the things is you sing about the things they think about most, but don't talk about. That becomes an emotional outlet for the people, and they feel they have a friend in the song. They like it, they buy it, they play it, they sing it, because it's something that seems to fit their purpose.[10]

Hence one of the things the music does is to "name" or "show" or "display" feelings. The country fan knows "they are singing about me." This takes on added significance when one considers how working people tend to deal with their interior lives. Many, I think most, working people do not engage in psychobabble on a scale anything like that of college trained people. They don't typically have the highly differentiated language of literate discourse and do not focus on the interior of the self and personal subjectivity to the extent of most business and, especially, professional people.

This does not mean, of course, that feelings are unimportant. As Webb Pierce says "you sing about the things they think about most, but don't talk about." This is why country music can play such an important role in singing their feelings. But it does more than only sing them. It dramatizes them, it gives them importance, it intensifies them. It is not only that people like Roy Acuff or Patsy Cline or Hank Williams or Kitty Wells or Willie Nelson or Emmylou Harris or Garth Brooks or Kathy Mattea sing the same things you think about, it says to working people: "You're not crazy. Other people have these feelings too. You are not alone. You've got company, and important company at that." Moreover, if these things can be performed on the air or in concert, this is big-time stuff!

Still, there is another dimension to this matter of feelings, and it is even more deeply related to class. It has to do with the status of the feelings of working people in the wider culture. Arlie Russell Hochschild observes "high-status people tend to enjoy the privilege of having their feelings noticed and considered important. The lower one's status the more one's feelings are not noticed or treated as inconsequential. The feelings of the lower-status party may be discounted in two ways: by considering them rational but unimportant or by considering them irrational and hence dismissible." She also argues for a corollary of this doctrine of feelings: "The lower our status, the more our manner of seeing and feeling is subject to being discredited."[11]

We have already seen that working-class taste is a dominated aesthetic. We need to understand that it is a dominated affect as well. What country does in this context is to "show" the marginalized feelings of working people's lives. To have your feelings sung and in a style that bespeaks your own taste—in fact celebrates it—takes on an importance of the first order. It is difficult to exaggerate and hard to understand adequately the portent of this because it runs culturally deep in a host of working-class practices that are not highly visible. It is a hunger of soul.

Jack Maxey is a United Methodist pastor who loves country music and sings and plays it on his guitar. He is quick to say that he is not Hank Williams, but who is? One day he was preparing a sermon on loneliness using a text from the Psalms. He came up with the idea that he would begin the service by singing "Amazing Grace." Later, right before the sermon, he would sing Hank's "I'm So Lonesome I Could Cry." Then he would preach about the loneliness theme from the psalm and amplify it with the country song. At the end of the service he would ask the congregation to sing "Amazing Grace" again, but this time to the tune of "I'm So Lonesome I Could Cry."

The lyrics of the one and the music of the other go together very well. When he did this on Sunday morning, he was met by a woman after the service who had waited until everyone was gone to have a private moment with him. She said: "I have been going to this church my whole life and I have had a hunger that has simply never been fed. Today this service touched me and fed me in a way I have never known."

The Expression of Working-Class Taste

So far I have suggested basic dimensions of working-class taste, pointed out with Bourdieu that it is a dominated aesthetic, argued that elitist taste legitimates social inequality, and in the section immediately above intimated how important it is to see one's feelings in a dominated affect not only expressed but done so in a working-class taste that venerates and celebrates them. Since working-class taste has received a good deal of attention previously, it will not require as much development here. But it would be a mistake to miss the importance of taste and its expression as a fourth aim or good of the music. It is not extraneous to it, it is not accidental, it is central to the goods of the music itself.

I prefer to examine this question by looking at one of the most grotesque examples one can find of working-class taste in the television show, *Hee Haw*. The setting of the show is almost exclusively rural, but it will do all the same. I also don't doubt that it was always profit oriented. Yet, something is going on there about taste that is so deeply cultural, it is clear in spite of the bizarre trappings of the show.

Hee Haw is done by country music artists almost entirely, except for guest appearances by those outside the field, and it could hardly be more stereotypical. It is a burlesque of rural working people. It is filled with corn-liquor-drinking/slothful/bib-overall-dressed men and mini-short-jean/plunging-neckline/bosom-busting-out women. It displays folk lying on the ground with their jugs and bloodhound dogs, and portrays unbridled ids in sanitized humor.

What in the world goes on here? Several things come through as I enjoy the show. For one it makes rural taste so extreme that anyone can set up camp this side of it and be okay. "Maybe I do like country music and maybe I'm not a sophisticate, but I'm not like that!" The mocking of an extreme can legitimate its more moderate expression. But it was more than that. Again, the humor, the parody, the knee-slapping, foot-stomping, belly-laughing humor all conspire to say, "We know this ain't real. It's just fun." But this too expresses something of the "rowdy and loud at the Twist and Shout."

Yet even more than this, the moments come when something is done that is clearly a highly competent country music performance. Think here of Roy Clark's regular appearances and his virtuoso guitar work. Not many people "pick" guitar better than Roy Clark. In one of those intricate, strenuous (one might even say athletic) performances he would look into the camera, smile, and stick his tongue out of the corner of his mouth as if to say "this is hard and I have to concentrate to do it," but you know Roy can do it, and do it with a flair. Sticking the tongue in the corner of his mouth makes the virtuosity down-home, keeps the performance humble, and re-establishes Roy as "one of us." It is a reconnection with working-class taste; it is a clear indication that he has not got uppity, has not got "above his raisin'." He's good, real good, but he "ain't showin' out in a way that puts him above us."

Even more important, it means Roy can be true to his kind and still be "awful good." There may be few things in working-class taste as important as being masterful and being one of us. To be good enough to work in the dominant discourse, the dominant aesthetic, the dominant etiquette, the dominant arts and then refuse it in order to be with your own people is near the height, if not the peak, of the working-class struggle for dignity. With this, to be uncommonly good in a common way is the dream of working-class taste.

Country music in a host of expressions climbs these heights.

A Living Expression

Like other music, country is a tradition. In the main it is a tradition of rural and urban working-class U.S. Americans. It is constituted of a range of practices of composition, performance, and enjoyment. These have been honed and extended across its almost eighty-year commercial history in the United States. Criteria and standards have emerged for its evaluation not only in composition and performance but also in the critical evaluations of its fans. Its practitioners and followers have developed discerning judgment, trained perceptions, and complex forms of appreciation.

As a tradition, country music serves a range of goods or aims. At its best it does not seek these goods in some utilitarian sense, but rather serves them in an intrinsic sense, that is, in the very practices of the music these goods are embodied. The music is not merely a means to the ends of the music but a living expression of the ends when done well. In its intrinsic fulfillment of the most basic of these aims country music embodies working-class life, makes the ordinary important, dramatizes and intensifies the feelings of a dominated affect, and expresses working-class taste. While certainly not exhaustive, these are among, at least, the most important dimensions of its working-class sensibilities.

But we are not done. In its embodiment of working lives the music reflects the trapped dimensions of the working world, the powerful contradictions that haunt the everyday lives. It faces these with as much forthrightness and grittiness as any music. We begin an examination of these next.

PART III

The Contradictions and the Politics of Resistance in Country Music

Chapter 5
Tradition, Modernity, and the Wild Side of Life

Ray was just about my favorite cabdriver. He exuded charisma, and anyone who came to the cabstand would sit and just listen to him by the hour. To be there when he was "on stage" was to live always with his memory burned into your mind. Sometimes he just talked, or told jokes, but at his best he told stories and sang. One of his favorite "performances" was to sing and then do a bridge in the song by playing a Coke bottle in the fashion of blowing into a jug. He especially liked country music variations on the blues.

Yet beneath his warmth and smile there was a fury in Ray, a defiance that I was quite frankly afraid of. I loved him but I never wanted to cross him. I can remember those slights and indignities that cabdrivers experience as commonly as the shifting of gears in a car. When he could not express anger about such commonplace injuries, his face would redden until I thought he would explode. The local newspaper editor once implied directly, albeit in a jovial mood, that Ray would never leave the cab business because he had no ambition. This was a good customer of Ray's who admired him and who represented no little income each week. Ray could not vent his feelings against the man without serious financial consequences, but he virtually shuddered in stifled rage.

Ray both loved and hated that small Mississippi town. It was home and he knew a "thousand" people there. They liked him or at least admired him, but his life was long hours of driving a cab punctuated by "performances" and daydreaming. He always hoped for some break, some new opportunity that never came. He hated the town because he understood that there really was nothing there for him. Driving a cab was something you did on your way to someplace else. Ray never knew where that was.

Once he joined the army to try to get away. To put Ray in the army was like placing a catfish in a glass of water. He returned home within three months with four fingers missing on his left hand, the result of "an accident" he had with a table saw. When asked about it, Ray gave off an almost maniacal smile and simply said, "It's the fastest way out of the army."

A fastidious sort, he always smelled like Mennen and his skin virtually beamed with the careful scrubbing he did every day, a practice not shared by all cabdrivers. He wore dress slacks, not wash pants, and usually a silky shirt that he left open down to the middle of his chest, a stylistic touch most men could not get away with in a time and place of tough-guy masculinity.

Ray was a handsome man, and women adored him. Often they would call and ask for him personally to pick them up. He maintained a busy sex life with at least a dozen women in that small town. Even as a teenager with fulminating hormones I wondered not only how he initiated so many liaisons, but also how in hell he kept them all "current." Still, he talked of finding "the right one," a woman he could really love.

Then he fell in love with Margie, a woman who owned a small, struggling store on the wrong side of town. Ray changed. He stopped his womanizing. He spent all his free time with Margie. Suddenly his blues songs on the Coke bottle turned into love songs. He gave happy renditions of "I'd waltz across Texas with you." Within a matter of days his music went from "Born to Lose" to "My Happiness." As the months wore on, they made plans to marry.

Margie lived in the back of her store, which was stifling hot in the summer. To make her comfortable and so they could later share it together, Ray ordered a $50 window fan for her place. This was a sizable purchase for Ray in those days, but he stringently saved for the fan, which would come C.O.D.

One day when Ray was supposed to be out of town on a cab

trip, he returned early and dropped by the store. Margie was in the back bedroom and so erotically engaged with another man that neither of them heard Ray until he stood in the doorway.

I don't know why that happened. Margie was known to be a very smart woman. She hated that store, but as marginal as it was, it was the best bet she had to make a living. She was trapped there. Some people said that the quickest way out of a life like that was whiskey or sex, and Margie didn't drink. Perhaps she knew that she and Ray had no future. Perhaps both of them had been damaged too much to form and keep an ongoing relationship. Margie always wanted more. There was always something she wanted to be that she had never been. Sex was the best way she could deal with that.

The next day the fan arrived. I remember the pain of watching Ray pull two twenties and a ten from the inside compartment of his wallet and hand them one at a time to the delivery man. He then slowly opened the box, took out the fan and set it on the floor. A soft breeze blew through the cabstand and a pasteboard ticket wired to the handle of the fan was the only thing in the room that moved. Ray just stared at his purchase.

A local building contractor finally broke the silence:

"Ray, I'll give you $15 for that fan," chuckling as he said it and knowing full well the vulnerability of his prey. His laughter gave a vicious edge to what had to be the cruelest thing I ever saw of that kind.

"I'll take it," Ray shot back, flashing with anger and giving the contractor a look of abject disdain but also of a don't-give-a-damn defiance that would not be deterred even by so heartless and insensitive an offer.

"I'll give you $50, Ray, plus postage," intervened my father in what was one more instance of the kind of humanity I had come to associate with him. With that my dad went to the money purse in the cabinet and counted out the $50 in bills and the postage in change.

That was Wednesday. On Friday night Ray was driving until midnight, and I had the all-night shift. Nothing was going on, and we spent virtually the entire evening talking.

Margie's name never came up. Instead, we talked abstractly about life and death. In the hour before he went home, we talked about murder and suicide, coming to the mutual conclusion that we could understand how someone might under rare circumstances commit murder, but that neither of us could comprehend how anybody could commit suicide.

After going home myself about 5:00 A.M., I came back about 9:30 because I couldn't sleep and started answering the phone. I had not been there ten minutes when the phone rang and an urgent voice told me:

"Tex, your dad needs to get down here right away and get Ray's cab. It doesn't look good being here. Ray's shot and killed Margie and he's shot hisself in the head. He ain't gonna live neither they think."

The ambulance passed within fifty feet of the cabstand and I could see through the frosted lines of the back windows the faintest outline of a body convulsing and thrashing. Ray died fifteen minutes later at the King Daughters Hospital.

At the time I was devastated by the loss of Ray and the unexplainable killing of Margie and of himself. It was one of those things that made no sense. I often experienced this business of things not coming together, of people who loved and hated Brookhaven, who wanted to stay there and wanted to leave, who hated to go and hated to stay. Ray's defiant rage and the way he sat on it was not an exceptional experience for me, but one common to the people I knew best. I had contact with dozens of people like Ray and Margie longing for a traditional relationship of love and commitment and at the same time living on the wild side of life. We all sang about love and wanted love, as much as anything, but it seemed so hard to find for many people and so hard to keep when finally found. And women, we damn near worshiped them, on the one hand, and then to see such acts of violence, on the other, or to hear jokes or comments so utterly demeaning to them. Moreover, it was often the case that a very able woman like Margie was trapped in a world she could not escape.

The story of Ray and Margie does not focus on the whole issue of racism and segregation, but this was one more crazy contradiction. My real name is Tex; it is not a nickname. I was named after a black woman, Texanna Gillham. To get your name from a woman who represents a stifled and oppressed people and to grow up in that kind of segregated world is an experience where you are continually caught up in strange inconsistencies of the first order. But such things came with the territory.

For all the years I continued to live at home I was cooled by that fan on long, hot summer nights, a constant reminder of the strange events that befell Ray and Margie. In that time I did not know what a social contradiction was, at least not by name. Yet I experienced this sense of life not coming out right over and over again. In fact, it seemed that opposites so often came in the same package. We fought what we wanted even in the moments when we desperately sought it.

Across the years I have come to believe that these events reflect much larger realities than the quirks of individuals alone. Much more systemic forces are afoot. These contradictions are deeply writ into the social makeup of class life and other social and cultural dimensions of lived existence in the United States. I do not mean only a logical contradiction. Rather I mean something lodged in the concrete lives of working people, a contradiction where things do not come together in the everyday practices of working-class life. In a word, they are structural.[1] In saying this it is not my intent to suggest that Ray—or Margie in her infidelity—was free of responsibility for his life and his lethal outburst, but to call attention to the world in which their lives were lived and to name deep fault lines that lie in wait for travelers across a turbulent terrain.

There is no more basic way that country music embodies working-class life than in the way it expresses the contradictions of that uneven world. Once one begins to listen to the music with attention directed to contradictions, they seem to occur everywhere, so much so that one is tempted to call country the music of contradiction.

The story about Ray and Margie reflects many, not all, of these contradictions. In the next two chapters I want to look at six of them, especially those of working-class life and the way these are reflected in country music.

Tradition and Modernity

Dan Seals sings a song called "Five Generations of Rock County Wilsons" about the selling of the last fifty acres of the traditional homeplace of the Wilson family. Some of the family returns to make the sale ("strange men who wore suits in the summer . . . trying to hold their maps in the wind"). Some of those there smiled and some didn't, says the song, but "none of 'em came back again," and after five generations "the last fifty acres apparently didn't mean a damn thing to them." Soon the "big diesel cats" are tearing up the woods where the singer of the song used to play. This is the land "where my mama and her mama laid," and the singer is glad his mother isn't there to see this fundamental betrayal. The song ends when the singer gets onboard a Greyhound bus and "was gone." With a sense of ambiguity, it is unclear whether the singer of the song was thoroughly opposed to the sale of the land and fought it or whether he was one of those men "who wore suits in the summer," and at least in the final outcome was one for whom "the last fifty acres apparently didn't mean a damn thing."[2]

There is a deep contradiction in this song: the heartbreaking loss of something that will never return and the necessary leaving of Rock County, which is as inescapable as the pain. How can you leave a place that is as poignant in meaning as Rock County seems to the singer?

Because you have no choice.

Perhaps not every last person is forced, but the overwhelming majority is displaced. Over the course of this century a shift of historic scale occurred. The movement in the United States from a rural society and agrarian economy, especially in the South, to an urban and industrial one represents mammoth social change. The more recent shift to a services economy and now increasingly to an electronic one heightens the magnitude of such change. The loss of traditional patterns, the emigration from farm to city and from one section of the country to another, the geographical and social dislocation, the emergence of new forms of living, the changing of cultural commitments, the reshaping of the inequalities of the society, the struggle over moralities, and the search for religious and spiritual focus are encoded in working people and chronicled in country music. It would be strange if country music did not reflect such events.

In the song about Rock County Wilsons the singer simply cannot understand his life apart from Rock County. It is the hallowed ground of his ancestors and a place where he obviously holds profound roots and deep moral connections. The lyrics speak a bitterness about the "damn" lack of meaning it had "to them," and the singer turns out to be one of "them." This illustrates the systemic nature of contradiction because here two structural characteristics fuse, but are in opposition to each other, in this case the characteristics of tradition and modernity. He is a Rock County Wilson, and he has to leave. His identity and his life are fused but in opposition to each other.

It could be said, however, that this is not a real contradiction but the case of a person with an antiquated identity who has not fully joined the modern world, that his identity is based in a time that is gone so that it is not a matter of structural contradiction but of nostalgia, on the one hand, and the realities of modern life, on the other. While such a view has some merit in country music (e.g., songs that are a bathos of sentamentality), it does not address structural properties at work in a song like this. The wide-ranging loss of land in the U.S., especially the gobbling up of small and middle-size farms, is real, and a good case can be made that it is not only not necessary but also deleterious.[3]

Moreover, to suggest that traditional life is dead requires that one ignore an enormous range of people and patterns in this society. While tradition of this kind may be a residual cultural form, and while traditional life itself is subject to change and does not look like its practice in the nineteenth and early twentieth centuries, it is nevertheless very real and a wide-ranging structural characteristic.

No more basic contradiction exists than that of tradition and modernity in country music. You do not have to look far to find a country song addressing this issue: "Daddy Sang Bass," "Whatever Happened to Old Fashioned Love," "Sign of the Times," "Luckenbach, Texas," "Me and You and a Dog Named Boo," "Outside the Nashville City Limits," "Tulsa Time," "Where Have All Our Heroes Gone?" and many, many more.

It would be a mistake, however, to see the music as only looking nostalgically at tradition and yearning for "the good old days." One Dolly Parton song notes that the good old days were bad.[4] Even in the same artist one finds both sides of the contradiction defended.

Taking a position opposite to that of "Five Generations of Rock County Wilsons," Dan Seals presents a searing indictment of the traditional hometown in a song entitled "They Rage On." The first two verses are about two young people in a small town. "She's a small town girl / with no room to grow / And he's a reckless boy with nowhere to go." They are caught in this setting "like birds in a cage / with no place to fly, . . . and they rage on."[5]

The second two verses turn to another older couple, and perhaps theirs is the destiny of the young couple of the first two verses. These two "meet in a rented room / on a crosstown street." Her youth is gone as are his dreams "but for a while they feel / like they used to feel / and they rage on."

The rage of both couples is "Against the lives that this world gave them / Hopin' somethin's there to save them." Both couples exist in these moments "somewhere between right and wrong / in the gray between dusk and dawn / they tell themselves they're not alone."

The chorus after each set of two verses intensifies the passing and loss of time and of opportunity. They are "Somehow searchin' for the answers / In the night like shadow dancers / Before their time is gone."

This is no idealization of tradition and the small town. It is a place of caged constraint with no opportunity, with no room to grow and nowhere to go. Time takes people who are young "with no place to fly" and turns them into couples who have lost their youth and dreams and in desperation try to feel "like they used to feel."

I am struck by the juxtaposition of hope and rage. They

seem at first so completely unrelated, but the result of unanswered hope is rage, until it becomes the self-loss of resignation. It is a hope that "somethin' in this world will save them" that makes it possible to rage on. But I get the sinking feeling in the song that it will not come. These are people caught in the backwaters of a changing world, in the small towns on the edges of life where people paper over the chasms of loss with ill-fated intimacies. Clearly this is not Rock County and these couples are not Wilsons, but maybe that's because the Wilsons left.

Still, contradictions inevitably find expressions in tensions that are often unresolved. While country music registers protest against the incarcerations of traditional life, it also takes issue, even more sharply, with modern life, with its temptations, its lack of moral depth, its surface satisfactions, and the short-lived durability of its grip on things that last.

It is not my intention here to side with the raging couples over against the Wilsons of Rock County but to name the contradiction and to leave it unresolved because that's the way the songs so often depict it. No better illustration of this exists than the song "Cadillac Ranch." It opens with a family in trouble with their farm. With a dry well, a cow in the same condition, and a bank about to foreclose, Mama has the idea of turning the place into a bar with the new name of "Cadillac Ranch." It becomes a very successful operation where "the only thing we raise is Cain." It is a strange new world for farm folk where "You don't need the sun or rain / Just neon lights and some ice cold beer / Keeps everything green [with money] around here."[6]

It seems too good to be true, and the song intimates as much. In the chorus it says: "Now we call it the Cadillac Ranch / We're parking cars in the old feed patch / There's a bar in the barn / And the place stays packed / Till the cows come home at Cadillac Ranch." One can argue, I suppose, that the ominous note at the end was put there simply to satisfy some of the more traditional fans of country, but whatever the reason, many working people simply do not trust money-making moves like that of the song and believe that "the cows will come home." It is hardly a veiled note of judgment. Such things do not work out in a traditional world. They smack too much of the fancy frills and fragile facades of modern life. They are not reliable. You cannot finally count on them.

One can, of course, understand the line about the cows coming home differently. It can be seen as a kind of anticipation that the bar is temporary, a coping and survival move until the farm operation itself can be reinstated. But it seems too lucrative, and the farm situation too dismal for such an eventuality. It can also be viewed as an even larger commentary on the farm situation nationally—that we cannot get by continually by turning from the substantive enterprises that sustain life to the ephemeral profit-making, short-lived ventures based on booze, entertainment, and dance. In this sense the Cadillac Ranch becomes a symbol for modern life itself, based in nothing that endures and occupied with a triviality that does not finally count.[7]

Country music receives no little criticism for its preoccupation with traditional life and with the past. Accusations of nostalgia and sentimentality populate commentaries about it, and certainly the central role of the contradiction between tradition and modernity provide only more ammunition for such critique. It poses the question of why tradition and the past are so important in country music and to working people. Let me add, however, that people who make such comments usually have an astounding lack of awareness of the degree to which they are accommodated to modernity and a complacency about its direction that more than rivals that of most traditionalists.[8]

Walter Ong claims that traditional and oral people do not live in the past but use the past to serve the present.[9] His comment is on target, and an understanding of the music and working people will be more clearly displayed if one works from this perspective rather than from one that sees the music and the people as unthinking, committed publics of cultural lag.

For one thing, tradition serves the present by helping to make sense of what working people are up against. Until the last twenty-five years most working people in the United States came out of rural and small-town America, and many still do. Popular culture and especially country music "map" people's cultural and historical lives. It tells them who they are and where they come from. The celebration of tradition in country music speaks directly to this concern.

More than that, the focus on tradition helps working people cope with the challenges of modernity and working-class existence under capitalism. This focus preserves forms of life and commitments facing the erosion of contemporary social change. Anthony Giddens observes that "one does not have to be a primitivist to see that . . . capitalism has . . . stripped away a massive variety of institutions, skills and forms of human experience, many of which are now irretrievably lost." He calls for "a philosophical anthropology" that "must attend closely to what we can retain of the human diversity that is being devoured by the voracious expansion of . . . capitalism."[10] As populated with commercial interests as country music is, it serves to hold on to working-class life, which is in itself a profound embodiment of the contradiction we have in view.[11]

Traditional Morality and the Wild Side of Life

Closely related to the contradiction of tradition and modernity in country music is that of traditional morality and the wild side of life. Expressions of traditional morality can be found throughout the history of country music.

Alongside this exoneration of the traditional is an equally long and, perhaps, even more extensive list of songs that address the wild side of life. Jimmie Rodgers both sang and epitomized the "ramblin' man" who could not stay put and could not live up to traditional life ways. In "Blue Yodel" he is going to get a pistol "as long as he is tall" and shoot Thelma "just to see her jump and fall."[12]

The honky-tonk music that emerged in the thirties has had a place in country ever since. It is perhaps the purest expression of the hard living, the slippin' around, the loneliness, the heartbreak, the despair, and, not to be missed, the celebration of the wild side of life. Michael Bane described the honky-tonk for Saturday night regulars.

91

That raunchy, neon-lit bar with its cheap beer and even cheaper solace is called home . . . as American as apple pie. . . . A working-class pitstop between today and tomorrow; a buffer zone between exhaustion and despair; soft lights and hard country music—a good honkytonk is all that and more. [13]

Arguably, the most famous country songs deal with themes of hard living, honky-tonks, and the wild side of life. Among the best are Ted Daffan's "Born to Lose," Webb Pierce's "There Stands the Glass," Lefty Frizzell's "If You've Got the Money I've Got the Time," Hank Williams's "Honky Tonkin'" and "Hey, Good Lookin'," Hank Thompson's "The Wild Side of Life," Kitty Wells's "It Wasn't God Who Made Honky Tonk Angels," Waylon Jennings's and Willie Nelson's "Good Hearted Woman" and "Mammas Don't Let Your Babies Grow Up to Be Cowboys," Willie's "Whiskey River," and Garth Brooks's "Friends in Low Places," but this is a short list.

Closely related themes of cheating songs such as Floyd Tillman's "Slipping Around" and lost love songs like Ernest Tubb's "Walking the Floor Over You" all deal in one way or another with the loss of traditional morality and the coming of the roads, the cities, the honky-tonks, and the temptations of bright lights and illicit romance.

This contradiction, so prominent in the music is, if anything, even more prominent in working-class life. It is easy to "explain" traditional commitments as those of people who live in the past or who are "culturally delayed" or not "with it," but traditional commitments play no small role simply in coping and survival in the working-class world. When life is lived up against the wall, when you live close to the line, the family and other traditional institutions provide support and resources to face the vicissitudes of life.

Most women are a divorce away from poverty in the working-class world, and working men know that the family cannot make it on their income alone. It takes the family and the extended relationships it represents to make it, and country music knows it. Songs about the crucial role of family fall from country music like rain from clouds.

One often hears country music characterized as "conservative." While there are places where this is so, it is a misdirected characterization. Country music is more accurately understood as traditional rather than conservative. Strictly speaking "conservative" in political terms is a point of view in the United States that stresses liberty and the free individual, laissez-faire capitalism, the minimalist state, strong defense and antiwelfare social policy. It supports a competitive, free market where the individual is supposed to pursue self-interest so that the greatest good of the greatest number will emerge from the "natural" workings of unencumbered human striving. The basic threat to a conservative is the erosion of liberty.

This is decidedly not the traditional view. The emphasis is not on the competition of free individuals but the cooperation of basic institutions, like the family, the school, and the church. The basic commitment is not to liberty but to a religious and socio-moral world. Traditional life does not encourage the pursuit of self-interest but instead focuses on the restraint of self-interest and the solidarity of the community. It distrusts self-interest because of its capacities to disrupt the harmonies of communal existence. Finally, the basic threat is not the loss of liberty, but moral decay. When seen in terms of this distinction it is clear that the commitments of country music are with the traditional view.[14]

Most working people live on an interface of order and chaos. To cope, to survive, to maintain some semblance of order in a world where the money is short, where a reversal sends you into deep debt and the necessity of struggling with it from day to day and month to month means that you have to fight against the chaos. You have to be careful and watch out for threats that can disrupt small gains or send the family plunging into even deeper disaster. It means you have to work at a job you don't like, but hating the job only adds to the problem of keeping at it. The struggle for order in such a world is a consuming activity.

All this occurs in a larger culture of winning where the individual is blamed for failing to live up to the ideals of achievement and success. In this kind of world it is not surprising that many working people turn to "respectability" as a lifetime pursuit. It is a compensative goal, in part; one that is justified so often by comments like: "We may not be big shots, but we are a respectable family." "We ain't fancy, but we raised good kids and we work hard for everything we get." Still, it is not enough to see it simply as compensative. It also has to do with self-respect, with being able to hold your head up, with the feeling that you count, with a claim that you pay your own way and don't cheat to make it "the way so many of the rich folks do." It is being able to say, "at least I got mine the right way."[15]

What is not said usually is how difficult this lifestyle is. Oh, it is not hard perhaps for a few years. It seems right when you are full of dreams and love is young or at least the hope of it is. The problems come when the work becomes too predictable, too filled with the certainties of an eight-hour day or longer, and crowded with the same things and with other job options that look no different or worse. In the working world some of the men take on an extra job, and the women do a second shift at home.[16] The difficulties mount as life at home is the brief respite from work and the place where the dreams are continually tailored to fit the constraints of an attenuating hope. Too much work and too little gain, too much tedium and too little change, too much respectability and too little celebration have led many working people to sing Reba's song "Is This All There Is?"

For some the wild side of life beckons. So Hank Thompson can complain that he "didn't know God made honky tonk angels" and accuse the woman he alone truly loves of going back to "the wild side of life." In response Kitty Wells can puncture his claims with a theological comment that "it wasn't God who made honky tonk angels," but "too many times married men think they're still single that has caused many a good girl to go wrong."[17]

One should not miss the fact that the honky-tonk and the wild side of life represent a chance to live. While such temptation cannot be reduced to an escape from the tedium of working-class life, the desperation involved in these ventures should not be missed either. Willie Nelson can plead for a "Whiskey River" to "take my mind," and the song "Bubbles in My Beer" says it straight: "Oh, I know that my life's been a failure / I've lost everything that made life dear / And the dreams I once made now are empty / As empty as the bubbles in my beer." It is the time when Loretta sings that she has torn up the chicken coop where her man has "set" her while he had a good time. It's getting toward night and she is taking off "'cause now Mama's got the pill." And Ruby is taking her "love to town."[18]

Moreover, Jim Ault's research establishes the importance of traditional commitments in controlling male sociality. In a traditional world men have been central to avoiding chaos. They usually have been the "breadwinners," the ones with the marketable skills that were acceptable in the public world. But they have also been the main, though not the only, ones who walk out the door. This is one reason why self-interest is not vaunted in traditional teachings. If the man starts to seek his unrestrained self-interest, he may leave for the wild side of life. If he does, it means bedlam for the family.[19]

For this reason nothing is more threatening to traditional order than the wild side of life. If that silver-haired daddy and mama's crying eyes and the little brown church in the vale and the open country red schoolhouse represent the institutions of traditional order, then the honky-tonk, painted women, whiskey rivers, and carousing men represent those of a decadent, albeit alluring, chaos.

Dorothy Horstman points out that the honky-tonk is a man's world. While women are there, they are not wives and girlfriends and are not respected. Horstman observes that "male chauvinism is common to a great many country songs, but nowhere does it show itself more clearly than in the honky-tonk song." She states that not all honky-tonk music is "piteous," that some of it has "the sheer exuberance of Saturday night on the town—though usually at the expense of the female." For example, Lefty Frizzell can sing "If you've got the money, honey, I've got the time," but he adds: "But if you run short of money, I'll run short of time."[20] I shall return to the sexism in country music in the next chapter, but for now let us not miss how much Horstman's comments underscore the honky-tonk world as the realm of the action-seeking male who has turned from the steady reliability of the traditional world to the temptations and pleasures of the wild and chaotic side of life.[21]

Conclusion

Country music embodies working-class life, and nothing more clearly illustrates this than the contradictions sung and played in the songs. The history of country music parallels a major shift from a more traditional, rural, agrarian society to a commercial, urban, industrial/service/info-technological one. The fractures between these worlds rumble through the experience of rural and urban working-class life, and the contradictions between traditional order and modernistic change figure prominently in the concrete lived lives of working people and can be found abundantly expressed in any period of country music.

The struggle to cope and survive and, in some cases, prosper in a century of enormous change and geographical dislocation has thrown the working class back on its own resources of stability, especially in traditional institutions with their familial and communal support. But the constraints of life lived close to the edge, of work that is in the main unsatisfying, and of prolonged striving in personal and family life inevitably lead to the search for alternatives. For many, "breaking out" is a leap to the wild side of life, which is a basic challenge to traditional morality and a powerful temptation to male sociality. Both traditional order and the wild side of life touch the very heart of working-class dreams because there is no more profound yearning than the search for a place of moral integrity, on the one hand, and emotional satisfaction, on the other. While such notions in these terms may not be articulated in discourse by working people, they are known in the lived practices of a concrete existence and rehearsed in the performance and enjoyment of country music.

Ray and Margie live out these contradictions in full-blown tragedy. But it is a world millions of others know very well, even if not in such lethal finality. It is an encounter with a persistent and unyielding disjointed existence.

It should not be forgotten that other fault lines run through the working-class world. They involve contradictions around the disparities of romantic love, the struggle against and acquiescence to the dominant society, and the accommodation to the systemic incongruities of race and gender. We turn now to these.

Chapter 6
Defiance, Love, Gender, and Race

I t would seem that Johnny Paycheck sang the quintessential country song on defiance with "Take This Job and Shove It." Can there be a working person in the world who has not felt those sentiments exactly? To be able to tell your boss that you are "walking out the door" and that "you better not try to stand in my way" has probably been at least the fantasy of every working man or woman at some time or another. Mocking his bosses as "a regular, low-down dog," and "a fool" the singer is clear, or so it seems, that he's leaving.

The job itself must be pretty bad. He's "been workin' there / For nigh on fifteen years / Seen some of my best friends' women / Drownin' in a pool of tears," and "seen a lot of my kinfolks die." He's "had a lot of bills to pay," but the precipitating event seems to be that "my woman done left and taken all the reason I been workin' for." It is clear that the job holds little intrinsic satisfaction. Without the woman who took off, there is no reason to stay.

Defiance and Submission

If one sees this worker, however, actually shouting at his boss to shove the job and walking out the door, two crucial lines in the song have to be ignored. According to the lyrics, at least, the worker never finally delivers the defiant lines. Rather, at the end of verse 2 he sings instead what could be a prayer: "Lord, I'd give the shirt right off my back / If I had the guts to say . . . Take this job and shove it." Then, at the end of verse 3 he sings "Lord, I can't wait to see their faces / When I get the nerve to say . . . Take this job and shove it." He never actually says it to the boss! The title of the song misrepresents what the singer does.[1]

Why? Because if he is making good money, and if he tells off his boss and leaves, he may well be making half that amount, provided he can get a job. More recently with the loss of good paying jobs with benefits one now hears some say "I wish I had a job to shove." The contradiction of defiance and submission comes with the territory of numbing jobs, insecure wages, and blighted opportunity.

Sometimes songs are a mixture of defiance and plaintive testimony but with submission all the same. When Tennessee Ernie Ford sings "Sixteen Tons," he complains, on the one hand, that you get nothing for loading sixteen tons but "another day older and deeper in debt," but, on the other, the defiance comes in the lines: "If you see me comin', better step aside / A lot of men didn't, a lot of men died / One fist of iron, the other of steel / If the right one don't get you, then the left one will." Yet, with such claims the lyrics tell even Saint Peter not to call, "'Cause I can't go / I owe my soul to the company store." This is extraordinary submission, indeed.[2]

Often the defiance comes in the protest of working hard and never getting ahead. Surely Dolly Parton sings the experience of millions of office workers with her song "9 to 5." I am struck by the vitality of both the lyrics and the music in describing a working woman who jumps out of bed and into the shower where "the blood starts pumpin'." Then from "nine to five" she works at a job that "ain't gettin' by." For her "service and devotion" and for the use of her mind she gets no promotion. The work is about the boss taking but not giving. The worker is "just a step on the bossman's ladder."

Some lines depict "dreams that he'll [the boss] never take away" and waiting for a time when the tide will turn. There is hope that "there's a better life," but the final verse includes these lines: "It's a rich man's game no matter what they call it / And you spend your life puttin' money in their pocket." With the vitality of the music and the hope expressed in the lyrics I expect more, but the song ends with a definition of things as only a rich man's game. Perhaps this is not quite submission, but it is a view of life that emphasizes resignation. In the movie by the same title, the office workers rise up against the boss and put him in his place. This, however, is a Hollywood ending that does not deal with the far more resistant issues of class. There is no such rosy conclusion in the song.[3]

Many songs in country portray this contradiction of defiance and submission. It is a common experience of working Americans, and all three of these songs had an extraordinarily popular reception when they were first released and they continue to be played. As was said above, the working class does not so much explore as show. The display of defiance and submission involves a sharp recognition of the dead-end, structural character of many jobs, and the wide pattern of submission speaks not so much to personal lack of fortitude as to a realistic coping with a work world out of joint. The constraints of work and its dissatisfactions play a prominent role in what are the most widespread themes in country music, those of the joys and struggles of romantic love.

The Centrality and Vulnerability of Romantic Love

Jimmie N. Rogers's study, as I indicate in an earlier chapter, finds that 73 percent of the top ten country songs from 1965 to 1980 deal primarily with the theme of love. His subsequent research bringing the material up to 1987 continues to find country dominantly concerned with this theme.[4]

Romantic love is important in virtually any popular music. This is even more the case in a place like the United States where it has such high cultural valuation. I prefer to look at this theme, however, from a focus on social class, because romantic love in country songs epitomizes basic concerns in the working world.

It is hard to miss how important love is in country music. A host of songs suggest its centrality in the music: "Behind Closed Doors," "Waltz Across Texas," "I Don't Need the

Booze (to Get a Buzz On)," "Just the Way You Are," "Let Me Be There," "Love Me Tender." "Near You," and "He Stopped Loving Her Today" (he died) are just a few. But listen to Elvis in "All Shook Up": "My hands are shaky and my knees are weak / I can't seem to stand on my own two feet / Who do you thank when you have such luck? / I'm in love—I'm all shook up!" Or listen to a song recorded by Dolly Parton, among others: "You shake my nerves and you rattle my brain / Too much love drives a woman insane / You broke my will but what a thrill / Goodness, gracious, great balls of fire!"[5]

And Kathy Mattea sings the beautiful imagery of "Love Chooses You": "You're pouring through me like a warm rain fallin' through the leaves on a tree."[6] Her touching rendition of "Where've You Been" tells the story of a couple who "never spent a night apart / For sixty years she heard him snore." They wind up in different beds on different floors in a hospital. Stricken with Alzheimers, "Claire soon lost her memory / Forgot the names of family / She never spoke a word again / Then one day they wheeled him in / He held her hand and stroked her head / In a fragile voice she said / Where've you been / I've looked for you forever and a day / Where've you been / I'm just not myself when you're away."[7]

In these songs, too, one frequently finds a certain "grittiness" about sexuality. Here it reflects working-class taste and festivity, and the objection to bourgeois rationality and restraint is no where more evident than in the celebration of erotic expression. And the music is upfront about bodies and physical love. It is just flat candid about the pleasures of sexuality, as much so as any music. Its clarity here and its connection to romantic love are profoundly class related.

At least two class-specific reasons can be given for this centrality of romantic love in country music. First, working people do not generally use the highly differentiated language of more literate, college-trained people to describe their inward emotional states. This does not mean that they do not have feelings and emotionally rich ones at that. Neither does it mean that working people are inarticulate or simpleminded. It is rather a matter of the language practices of a social location and of a use of language especially represented by country music. As important an authority as Conway Twitty, speaking about males, says it well: "I like a song that says things a man wants to say and doesn't know how to say it."[8] Given the way men tend to deal with feelings and their expression in this culture, I suspect that Twitty is on the money. The difficulty most males have giving voice to their feelings permeates this culture. Moreover, in the more oral culture of working men, they do not focus on their interiors or do analysis the way middle-class people do.

While this is nuanced differently for women, nevertheless it is still very important. Reba McEntire says that she "tries to sing songs for women they can't sing for themselves." Loretta Lynn says she sings about "the things that people go through," and no one sings the lives of working women more consistently and over so long a time as Loretta. Finally, at Dottie West's funeral Kenny Rogers says of her: "She sang emotions." Gaillard says it well: Country music is "a relentless reflection of emotion."[9] The singing of country music thus plays one of its most important roles in expressing the feelings and emotions of working-class life.

Second, if the job stinks, if the future looks the same or even more bleak than the present—a scenario for many working people in the present economic situation—then the question becomes one of which dimensions of life have a chance to be important. If a good deal of the rest of life offers no significance, then what else is there? In circumstances like these, romantic love, finding the right person, finding someone who is your deepest friend, your life partner, and a passionate lover can become the most important thing in the world.

Please understand that I do not mean to reduce romantic love simply to a compensative dynamic. I happen to believe it is one of the three or four most important things in life, but if a job does not call forth your interests and strengths, if the money is short or close, if the opportunities are limited for other forms of personal expression, if the present is hard and the future looks no different, then love can easily take on a significance that towers above everything else. In the working-class world this often happens and country music reflects it.

The contradiction comes at the point of the vulnerability of something so central. And vulnerable it is. Just listen: "Lovesick Blues," "Cold, Cold Heart," "Walking the Floor Over You," "Heartaches by the Number," "Singing the Blues," "Wasted Days and Wasted Nights," "Blue Bayou," "Before the Next Teardrop Falls," and "Release Me" to name just a few of a longer list that could fill the rest of this book.

Lost love in country music takes on a rejection and a desertion that is existential in sweep. It is more than the loss of an infatuation. It is death, at least metaphorically. Larry Gatlin sings "Statues without hearts / Stones with no feeling / Playing out a part / Never feelin' what we say / Statues without hearts / Stones with no feeling / That's what we'll become / If we let love get away."[10] Lyrics like these testify to the centrality of love but also to the devastation brought on by its loss.

If it takes on such significance, if it is so highly valued, then why is it so fragile as it so often seems in the music? One answer, of course, is that if you place such emphasis on one very human venture and then load it with so many unrealistic expectations, it will inevitably fail. There is no little truth here especially in this culture, but such a view holds true across the culture and I want to look more specifically at the class realities instead.

Walter G. Muelder, my teacher, used to say "If the fodder gets low, the horses start to bite each other." It is a trenchant comment directly applicable to love relationships in the U.S. For decades now it is clear that household and domestic stability is powerfully affected by declining economic indices. Incidences of separation, divorce, and desertion tend to follow cycles of unemployment and financial hardship.

In the U.S. we tend to disregard the impact of economic factors in personal life. Yet, it looms in the society like the proverbial elephant in the room that everyone ignores. Even our very lives can be radically affected by falling economic indices. The Gallup Organization reported "a Johns Hopkins University study showing that each 1 percent rise in joblessness is accompanied by an increase of 37,000 deaths—including 27,000 fatal cardiovascular cases, 650 murders, and 920 suicides—plus 4,000 additional admissions to state mental hospitals and 3,300 more criminals sentenced to prison."[11]

Economic reversals like these tend to fall disproportionally on the bottom half of the society.

The impact of such things on household stability is well documented and has been so for decades.[12] The inequalities of class insinuate themselves into the relationships of love and render them unstable. This is a contradiction of the first order because the very patterns of inequality that make love so attractive and central leave it difficult to achieve or, at least, to sustain. During hard times the man will find it increasingly difficult to face his spouse. No matter how systemic the cause of the economic reversals he will blame himself, at least in his own mind. She often has all she can do with one job at work and another at home. The helplessness sinks in for both of them. The sheer hardship gives way to arguments, to drinking, to seeking solace somewhere else, to strained relations, to increasing barriers to communication, and to quiet desperation looking for escape. Even the best of marriages suffer under such economic tough times.

Women as Salvation and the Sexism of Country Music

The contradictions only deepen when one sees the importance of love between men and women and then examines the place that women have had not only in much of the music but in the industry as well. Perhaps one of the best ways to get at this issue is to quote two people whose words capture the contradiction of the place of women and the force of sexism in country music. First, Curtis W. Ellison maintains that "There is a parallel tradition in secular country music culture that relies on the motif of salvation but replaces the love of Jesus with the love of women."[13] It would be difficult to exaggerate the place of women in country music as the ones who make life worth living for men. A song like "There Goes My Everything" says it well: "There goes my reason for living."[14]

Second, sexism permeates country music and has done so throughout its history. One of the worst lines ever written in country music comes from Johnny Paycheck: "God made man for himself and he made you for me."[15] This from the man who in "Take This Job and Shove It" could sing: "my woman's done gone and taken all the reason I've been workin' for." How can a man value "his" woman as the intrinsic reason for working at a job that is so self-emptying and then see her as created by God to serve utilitarian purposes for the man? But this is the contradiction.

In our review of the history of country music we see how much the industry militated against the rise of women to stardom, providing them only backup roles to men. Even later, in the fifties and sixties, women clearly took a backseat to men. It required the independent strength of a performer like Patsy Cline to counter the inequalities. Following her, the important work of Loretta Lynn took on the established sexism of the industry. The doors finally began to open more widely in the eighties, but as this is written we are in a "hunk" period, a time when young male stars like Garth Brooks, Vince Gill, and Billy Ray Cyrus are getting airplay and mega-attention. The constraints are back with only female performers of the stature of Reba McEntire able to share the limelight equally with male stars.[16]

What are we to make of this? How can women who take on a virtual mythic status of salvation in the music be so persistently subjected to the structured social inequality and symbolically constructed exclusion of sexism? The industry argued early on that the traditional values of the audiences militated against women working alone and that women had to be seen as members of a performing family unit in order to be on the road. Later, the industry would argue and still does that the country fans are dominantly made up of women and that they buy the records and attend the concerts and prefer male artists. Such claims, even when they contain some accuracy, do not touch the active collusion of the industry in sexist practices.

Moreover, it is not enough to claim that the salvation motif regarding women is simply another case of the "pedestalization" of women, though certainly this can be found in the music. The class factor introduces another dimension to this question. When romantic love takes on the importance it does in the working-class life of men, the place of women as answers to male issues crowds out attention to the role of men as answers to women's issues, not to mention the answers to women's issues where men have little part. For example, if she is the only reason he is working, what is her purpose in life besides being his? What does she do if she hates her job at work and the one at home too? These questions do not arise very often in country music or in any other kind of music for that matter, unless it is written by women for women. Indeed, when one finds attention given to women's issues in country music, they primarily come from a masculine perspective.

To be sure, we must not forget the class circumstances of women and men in the working world. One reason so many working women show little sympathy for feminism is because it seems so distant from their lives. She has a better chance of finding the right man who can solve her problems (as unlikely as that may be) than she has to correct the way the system works. She may know far more about this in her bones, in the lived practices of everyday life than anyone else. The very idea that she is going to get work that pays enough for the kids, for housing, for health care, for food, for clothes seems to be the impossible dream. To think that her pay will equal that of a high-paying, traditionally male job is like believing she could land on the other side of the moon. Moreover, the slight increases in ratios of women's wages to men's in the working-class world is a consequence of the loss of pay by men, not the increase of wages by women.

A profound interstructuring of classism and sexism occurs in the working-class world. The contradiction between the mythic role of women as a source of salvation and the wide-spread sexism in country music manifests this social construction, and is inherent to its traditional ethos.

This contradiction also needs to be placed in the economic history of this century and its impact on the family and on male and female relations. Shifting economic arrangements have had a profound effect on the family with serious consequences for working people.

I am struck by the fact that each of the contradictions examined so far characterized the relationship between Ray and Margie. They both loved and were trapped in a small

Mississippi town, they struggled with a traditional morality and the wild side of life, they defied and submitted to a world they could not control, and they lived out a consuming search for romantic love with deadly vulnerability. Margie's trapped life, her violent death, and Ray's murderous and suicidal acts testify to the insidious systemic and personal destruction of a patriarchal order. If the overt tragedy and evil of their story makes it more visible, we should not miss the pervasive reality of such things in working life—indeed in all our lives—that are not always so conspicuous or dramatic. The more massive destruction is in the everyday lives of millions of people who do not shoot each other, but live in silent resignation to the principalities and powers of a world out of joint.

I use "principalities and powers" here with a particular intent, because I believe this New Testament language speaks to material and cultural realities, both visible and invisible, which unleash enormously destructive powers in the lived existence of anyone and, in terms of our subject, in the lives of working people.

From a theological perspective these truly are principalities and powers. One needs neither an angelology nor a demonology to account for the pervasive and systemic destruction wrought by distorted commitments, rapacious imbalances of power, the violative practices of dominant institutions, and the dehumanizing impact of social inequalities in the common life. Indeed, we do not contend with flesh and blood alone but with elemental powers of the universe, powers so systemically embedded in the full range of our lives that they take on an emergent reality larger than, more pervasive than, their manifestation in individual acts alone. Before closing this chapter, one more such contradiction requires our attention.

African Americans and Racism

Another contradiction in country music is that of the central place of African Americans in the U.S., especially in the South, and their important role in country music, on the one hand,

and the relative silence about both blacks and racism in the music, on the other. It is an astounding silence and the very stuff of which contradictions are made.

The importance of African Americans to country music is undeniable. I indicate the influences of black music on country and the contribution of instruments like the banjo in the appendix. Without black music, country music simply would not be country. Hank Williams was taught guitar by an African American, Rufe Payne, nicknamed Tee-Tot. Elvis Presley attributed powerful importance to black entertainers.[17] Deford Bailey was an early (1925) and longtime performer on the Grand Ole Opry, but was later dropped from the show (1941).[18] Charley Pride attained superstar status, although his promoters veiled his racial identity at the beginning of his career. These are only a few of the influences that could be named.

But the silence about racism in the music is even more prominent. McLaurin and Peterson report:

> Racial attraction, fear, prejudice, and discrimination are pervasive in America, and perhaps nowhere more so than in the South and among country music fans. Yet there is no candid discussion in the music of the many poignant situations that pivot on questions of race in America. Of the thousands of songs on the country music hit charts since World War II, probably no more than twenty mention race in any connection. [19]

It is not a complete silence, however, and important exceptions exist. "I Want to See the Parade" by Tom T. Hall tells the story of a man watching a civil rights demonstration. He is offended by it all when asked by a little girl, a stranger, to lift her up so she can see the parade. The man only realizes that she is blind when she asks him to tell her why her father hates these people so. Searching for an answer the man admits "it was pretty hard to find."[20] Such lyrics call into question the lack of any basis for prejudice and racism.

Merle Haggard, more often remembered for "Okie from Muskcogee," sings a song entitled "Irma Jackson," which deals head-on with and approvingly of interracial love.

While sexual relationships between blacks and whites are hardly new, this kind of up-front defense of loving relations between these two races takes on prophetic qualities in country music. Bobby Braddock wrote a song sung by Tanya Tucker called "I Believe the South Is Gonna Rise Again," which holds up a vision of black and white "hand in hand." There are other country songs that address these issues, but not many.[21]

Some country artists actively supported discrimination and segregation. People like Hank Snow, Tammy Wynette, and Marty Robbins all campaigned for the segregationist presidential candidacy of George Wallace.[22] Peterson reports that major record companies have not produced racist records since World War II, but that some, like "Welfare Cadillac," seem to have overtones about black welfare cheaters. Smaller companies have produced racist records that were distributed by the Ku Klux Klan and the White Citizens Council. "Such records were sold over the counter in the Atlanta F. W. Woolworth as late as 1967."[23]

Country music comes out of the working class. It began in the South where whites and blacks knew one another, worked with one another, and sometimes, in settings not under surveillance, played with one another. These were not equal relationships, but they were real. That there is so much silence about racism, so little attention given to it, and some active contribution to the bigotry by country music is incarnate testimony to the American dilemma and to the fusion and opposition of contradictory social structures.

It is not my intention here to scapegoat country music or white working people about racism or sexism. None of the classical or popular arts and certainly not the upper classes in the United States have courageous histories in combating these profoundly wicked social constructions. It is ever, it seems, the work of a small minority to call into question such systemic evils. Still, neither working people nor country music can ignore their own complicity in what, along with classism and sexism, are the ugliest commitments of the American heart and of the dominant institutions of this society.

Life Ain't Fair

Country music reflects working-class life in the United States. As such it embodies the contradictions of that world and the impact of the wider society. Indeed, the history of the nation in the twentieth century can be read in the development of the music. Beginning in the traditional society that was the South early in this century the music incorporates the songs of traditional people, including those still a part of this culture and tied profoundly to its practices and commitments. Working people are also a people of migration and dislocation in this century, a people entering a modern, industrial, and now postindustrial and info-technological society. It is a world with the temptations of the city, of bright lights, booze, and alluring relationships that challenge traditional morality with the fascination of the wild side of life. It is a world of demeaning work where the exclusions and discriminations of life on the downside lead to a defiant protest and a submissive resignation. The battle of the sexes vaunts women as the representatives of a secular salvation even as it seeks to control them. It is a world where the systemic racism of the larger society finds contradiction in a deafening silence about a race of people as inseparable from the working class and country music as human color is from the world itself.

These are, of course, not the only contradictions, but are among the most important ones. Furthermore, contradiction is basic to the way white working people experience the world. Country music somehow embodies this, and with the exception of the silence about race, displays these contradictions to the people who live them.

But working people are not mere flotsam on the river of life. They are not only shaped by deep-seated social influences and contradictions. They also fight back. They resist. They do not merely acquiesce to the dominant powers of this society. Perhaps the most interesting thing about working people is their ability to defy the dominant world. In the next chapter we turn to this resistance as it operates in the lives of working people and as it is expressed in country music.

Chapter 7
Country Music and the Politics of Resistance

I don't remember the first time it happened, but I remember it occurring so many times that my impressions of it are quite strong. In a classroom setting I would say "ain't" and be corrected by my teacher. Even before she told me, I knew it was "incorrect." We were taught by a fine group of female English teachers in the public schools I attended. Today I often marvel at the quality of the teaching we received in the forties and early fifties in that small Mississippi town. And I liked every one of my teachers and somehow always did well in English, at least as well as a boy could do and not take a lot of heat from the other guys after class.

But every time a teacher told me not to say "ain't" or corrected some other grammatical error of mine, I felt a kind of guilt or disloyalty in using correct English. At a reasonably early point, say the sixth grade, I had learned about number, tenses, conjugations, verbs, nouns, adverbs, and adjectives. Besides that I could "hear" when they were correct. I suppose I had a faculty for English. It was, however, even clearer that I did not have a "patriotism" for it.

It would take the insight of Pierre Bourdieu to help me understand what was going on. The vernacular of the working class can be helpfully understood as "a refusal to 'overdo it,' to conform too strictly on the points most strictly demanded by the dominant code." It is "a rejection of the censorship which propriety imposes." Moreover, to adopt the dominant style is a denial of identity and a form of consorting with the more highfalutin and powerful groups.[1]

It would be years before I realized that my "guilt" and my sense of disloyalty over using correct English were expressions of a refusal of the dominant discourse. In my youth and throughout most of my adult life I can remember a strange befuddlement in my relationship to things "proper," but it is only in my encounter with this refusal of the dominant code that it begins to make sense.

Equipped with this new insight, I now see an awareness in working people of the degree to which the body, etiquette, taste, affect, and language are targets of domination. When working people fight off these attempts and develop the alternatives of the vernacular, profanity, rowdy and loud taste, direct and up-front emotion, and soul music, they are engaged in a politics of resistance. It becomes an expression of dignity and a focus of loyalty.

Resistance and Country Music

As the embodiment of working-class life it would be surprising if country music did not exude this politics of resistance. Once you begin to look at and listen to country music as an art of resistance, it seems to leap out at every point. It rejects cultivated charm, sophisticated wit, and highbrow refinement. Curtis Ellison points out that even the name the Grand Ole Opry "is a deliberate, rustic burlesque of formal and classical music."[2]

In describing country humor Dorothy Horstman notes that country is "deliberately corny," not because its bearers "are unlettered and unknowledgeable and unsophisticated. It is corny precisely because they are sophisticated." Pointing out that the humor distinguishes between "real people" and "uppity people" Horstman contends that it is used as "a foil to urban stereotypes."[3]

All of my life I have known about the "Southern boy con." It amounts to playing dumb as a way of showing up a sophisticate. I heard the tales and saw that it worked so often that even now when I hear someone say "Well, I ain't too smart," my first thought is to go home and "lock up my goat," because I figure my protagonist is out to get it.

Resistance has a long history among country music artists. No more pervasive evidence for this exists than the relationship that exists between the performer and the audience. It is called the "sincerity compact" by Jimmie N. Rogers and denotes that the artist will maintain a relationship to the fans as "one of them." It is difficult to exaggerate this aspect of country music.[4]

In 1961 a Grand Ole Opry group of performers, including Patsy Cline, did a show at Carnegie Hall in New York. Before the performance Dorothy Kilgallen, a newspaper columnist who gained fame as an intellectual on the TV show "What's My Line?" attacked the show (without having seen it) as the epitome of primitive "po' white" folks with their lynchings, gun racks, and attacks on civil rights workers. (Kilgallen's sensibilities about class were hardly commensurate with her concern about racism.) Such snobbery and bigotry infuriated Patsy. She shot back at Kilgallen from a stage in Winston-Salem, North Carolina, and called Kilgallen "the Wicked Witch from the East." Given Patsy's facility with salty, primal Anglo-Saxon language one can readily guess what she called her in private. Then she offered: "At least we 'ain't standing on New York street corners with itty-bitty cans in our hands, collecting coins to keep up the opera and symphonies."

The show in New York went well with a virtually sold-out audience standing in appreciation and applause throughout the evening. At the "Dixie Jubilee" in Atlanta three days later, Patsy had a large and lively crowd, and the Carnegie episode was still on her mind. While she said "We were awfully proud of being that fur up in high cotton," she was concerned about being seen as having betrayed her country roots and having gone uptown and become highfalutin. She wanted the fans to know she was "one of us" and "didn't get above her raisin'." She said it straight out: "Ah love ya. This ain't New York but it's uptown. You talk about a hen outta a coop—I really felt like one up there, I'm tellin' ya. But you know what? We brought that country outta them if anybody did. They sittin' up there stompin' their feet and yellin' just like a bunch of hillbillies, just like we do. And I was real surprised. Carnegie Hall is real fabulous but, you know, it ain't as big as the Grand Ole Opry."[5]

The sincerity compact is a form of resistance. In it the performer says "I am real, I am one of you, and I am not about to get uppity. And it's us against all the other so-and-sos who put us and our music down." It is clearly resistance.

Social Resistance

John Fiske argues that resistance takes two forms in Western societies, social and semiotic.[6] The first has to do with direct attempts to resist the status quo and to change the socioeconomic system. Little of this is to be found in commercial country music, and its appearance in working-class history in the U.S. is sporadic. In the case of country music the reasons are doubtless attributable to the gatekeeping of industry producers who are not about to risk investment on such risky political ventures, even if they agree with them. Not many do. Moreover, disk jockeys in country music have a history of avoiding such issues, due in part to their own social locations and their vulnerability in station politics. One has to look hard to find institutional courage in the country music industry.

Courage can be found among composers and performers from time to time. I think particularly of Kris Kristofferson's release "Third World Warrior." It is a searing indictment of U.S. policy in El Salvador and Nicaragua and a defense of the revolutionaries, including communists, there. It received little airplay and hardly any attention from the industry. Only an artist of Kristofferson's stature could get such a release out to start with.[7]

More than this, one does not find much social resistance of a radical kind among working people themselves. This is not because they are right-wing extremists, as the bigoted stereotypes contend. Most working people in the U.S. tend to be moderate in their political point of view. As a group they are far less conservative than upper middle-class business and professional men (I do mean males).[8] In part, it relates to their own realistic grasp of what the possibilities are, but it is even more profoundly tied to commitments that do not follow the political continuum of right, middle, and left as typically understood in the United States. This will get attention below. For now, it is enough to observe that social resistance gets little play, except sporadically, among working people, and especially in country music.

Everyday Resistance

The place of semiotic resistance is quite different according to Fiske. Semiotic resistance finds expression in identities, pleasures, and meanings. While social and semiotic resistance are certainly related, each is relatively autonomous; and popular culture functions primarily, though not altogether, in semiotic resistance. Against the tendencies toward homogenization, semiotic resistance will express difference. Against tendencies toward consensus, it will express conflict. It fights against incorporation into the larger culture. It resists imposed, external meanings by making its own claims for a distinctive set of meanings, pleasures, and identities.[9]

I am going to call Fiske's semiotic resistance "everyday resistance," both to use a simpler word and also to avoid what can be the reduction of everyday resistance to an abstract notion of "sign." Such resistance does indeed take place in alternative identities, pleasures, and meanings, but it is expressed in a host of everyday acts and practices not reducible to signals of resistance alone.

One of the best places to see this kind of resistance in country music is in the opposition to attempts to make the music more palatable to a wider public. This opposition has a history. The fight against the Nashville Sound is a good case in point. At a time in the late fifties and early sixties when the music was losing its traditional cast to the Nashville Sound, along came artists like George Jones, Doc Watson, Merle Haggard, and Loretta Lynn to oppose the absorption of country into pop music.[10]

In 1974 when Olivia Newton-John, an Australian pop singer who knew hardly anything about country music, was named top female singer by the Country Music Association, a number of important people in the business began a short-lived organization to counter this betrayal. More recently, the emergence of the neotraditionalists is clearly an opposition to countrypolitan and contemporary country music.

Even so, the most potent expression of such resistance is in the performance of the music itself. Hank Williams, Jr., for example, is a textbook case of such resistance. Ellison reports that a Hank Junior concert "luxuriates in a tone of relentless aggression." Suggesting that "in some respects, the music is secondary," Ellison describes the scene in ritualistic terms as an "intensive bonding around a popular culture of defiance."[11] See, for example, his songs "Family Tradition" and "All My Rowdy Friends Are Coming Over Tonight."

The assertion of working-class taste and being "rowdy and loud" at the "Twist and Shout" are also instances of everyday resistance. The literary critic Mikhail Bakhtin in his studies of the lower classes at the end of the Middle Ages demonstrates the many ways that festivity can be used as a popular form of criticism and resistance. Such festivity can "make possible and . . . justify the most extreme freedom and frankness of thought and speech."[12] It can cancel hierarchies, expose and undo pretension. Mockery, derision, and debasement are basic to its work. It has a deep suspicion of "official truth" and of the "official world."[13]

Garth Brooks's "American Honky-Tonk Bar Association," for example, takes on problems with pay, taxes, welfare, and the direction of the nation. It praises the "over-taxed, flag-wavin', fun-lovin' crowd / Their heart is in the music / And they love to play it loud."[14] The mixture of flag waving and criticism of the nation should not be missed here, an issue to be addressed below, but the use of festivity as the place to do such criticism is a basic form of resistance.

Everyday resistance, however, does not always take this kind of overt form of defiance. As Fiske indicates: "While accepting the power of the forces of dominance, it focuses upon the popular tactics by which these forces are coped with, are evaded or are resisted."[15] This takes any number of forms in country music, some of which we address above.

For one, the pleasure of participating in, listening to, dancing to, being a fan of country music are all examples of what de Certeau calls creating a "space apart" from the dominant culture. A space apart is an active form of resistance to the dominant culture that takes place while under the eye of the powerful. As de Certeau asserts, the relatively powerless can create a space, an opening where difference can be enacted, where the marginal can be "other," and where a different order can be celebrated and enjoyed.[16]

Country music does precisely this for many working people. This space apart becomes one where pleasure can be relished. Sometimes these are the pleasures celebrated in the music itself: "Nobody knows what goes on behind closed doors." Most times it is the pleasure of listening to country as "our" music, not "theirs." It is having the nerve to say "And if the sonsabitches don't like it, they can stick it where the sun don't shine!" In this kind of resistance it doesn't mean a damn thing if the wider culture doesn't like it. So much the better. Furthermore, it is even better if they don't understand it.

Something of this kind of resistance can also be found in the way that country fans treat their favorite performers when they are down on their luck or in deep trouble. Ellison takes note of the fact that when George Jones struggled through the worst days of his life, sick and weighing only 105 pounds, his record sales went to an all-time high.[17] There is an affinity with this kind of trouble, an identification with it and the person going through it. To stick with them is its own kind of resistance, especially when it cuts across the grain of certain established conventions. The response to people like Hank Williams and Patsy Cline in their personal struggles and early deaths further testifies to the power of this dynamic.

Country music is often stereotyped as "a tear in my beer" music, and as "somebody done somebody wrong" songs. While there is no question that country is a music made up in no little part of sad songs, we need not forget that a basic form of resistance is music as protest, as a "shouting of one's suffering."[18] I realize that such music can become a maudlin wallowing in self-pity, and it is frequently characterized in such terms. Even so, one does not have to defend the worst expressions of a tradition of music in order to name the best of it.

Views that see only a wallowing of self-pity in country music, however, usually come from people writing out of positions of privilege. It is questionable how much in touch they are with the kind of numbing that occurs in the working-class world. Such numbing may not come in the first few years, but it can finally get to you. Work takes the talking out of you.[19]

Walter Brueggemann points out the importance of lament in breaking numbness. The music plays a vital role in this regard. It shouts suffering, it laments, it opens up a space, it breaks the numbness, and often insinuates hope into situations of despair. He also maintains that grief is "the ultimate criticism."[20]

Merle Haggard's "If We Make It Through December" is a song about a man who is laid off at Christmas and wishes it could be a better time because he wanted the season to be "better for his little girl." It is a sad song, but he also hopes for a better time and a warmer climate in the near future. The lament is clear, but it breaks the numbness and opens the possibility of a new and different future.[21]

These are only a few instances of the kinds of resistance Fiske calls semiotic. Illustrations of this can be found in rich detail throughout country music. It is not a difficult search. Yet most of the illustrations above are from male artists and from songs from a man's perspective. We need to look at the ways that women have expressed resistance in a growing mass of songs in the tradition.

Women and Resistance

Given the backseat relationship women have had in country music throughout most of its history and given the characterization of the forms of resistance in focus here as those of the marginalized, it would be expected that women would provide sharp renderings of this. Such an expectation is not met with disappointment.

A good place to begin such an exploration is with an artist who may seem unlikely—the Grand Ole Opry comic Minnie

Pearl (Sarah Ophelia Colley Cannon). A star from 1940 until the 1990s on the Grand Ole Opry, she came from a well-to-do Centerville, Tennessee, sawmill family. Her character was a "blend of brash and bashful," of "the man-hungry old maid with a coy demeanor and glint in her eye," of "the homely wall flower with . . . pluck and grit," of "the small-town gossip without malice," always "bubbling with news of Uncle Nabob, Aunt Ambrosy, Brother, Lizzie Tinkum, and the other characters who inhabit her fictional Grinder's Switch neighborhood."[22]

When Minnie Pearl broke into the Opry as its only female performer, she was, as she said later, "the first woman to scramble with my fingernails up the side of a wall to try to get some recognition in a man's world."[23] To make it in that world a woman had to play by the rules but "playing by the rules" does not do justice to the "mobile infinity of tactics" that powerless groups and, in this case, women, have to employ.[24] "Playing by the rules" suggests much more conformity and complacency than the struggles marginal people experience.

The "wisdom" at the Opry was that a woman star would create problems for men in the audience with their accompanying wives or women friends if they looked too enamored with a beautiful artist. Her "man-hungry rube comic routine" built itself around the "deliberate cultivation of a sexually nonthreatening image." Further, she continually and craftily downplayed her two years at a finishing school before coming to the Opry. The success of someone like Minnie Pearl is testimony to the capacity to cope and find a way when all opportunity seems closed.

Such coping is a form of resistance to the powers that be. It is the finding of a niche, of course, but it is also a way of staying in contention, of fighting against the odds. Sometimes such efforts draw no little fire from those who contend it is demeaning and a violation of the integrity of the self. You would, however, be hard-pressed to sustain such a claim with an effort like that of Minnie Pearl. When the Opry stars appeared at Carnegie Hall, she was made spokesperson for the group because they knew she could handle it. Bufwack and Oermann call her "the Opry's mother confessor, chaperone, and good will ambassador."[25] To resist dominant power by tactically fulfilling a stereotype to the point of its laughable unreality is a resistance of the first order.

Efforts like Minnie Pearl's lead one to appreciate all the more the work of Kitty Wells and her hit "It Wasn't God Who Made Honky Tonk Angels." In 1952 it was the first big hit by a female artist since Patsy Montana's "I Want to Be a Cowboy's Sweetheart" in 1935, and sold more than a million copies.

Actually, in her personal life, Kitty was not the one from whom you would expect such a record. Married to the country artist Johnnie Wright, she put his career first and was herself a traditional wife and mother. After deciding to retire and focus her attention fully on the family she was asked to do the answer song to Hank Thompson's piece wherein a woman is blamed for leaving a relationship: "I didn't know God made honky tonk angels / I might have known you would never make a wife / You gave up the only one who ever loved you / And went back to that wild side of life."[26]

Her song in response touched a deep unsettledness among women who were fed up with the way things were going in post-World War II America. Kitty said it for many: "It wasn't God who made honky tonk angels / As you say in the words of your song / Too many times married men think they're still single / That has caused many a good girl to go wrong!"[27] This may seem mild now at the end of the century, but in the fifties the song was banned by NBC. The Opry, with typical caution, forbade Kitty to sing it on the radio. This, in spite of the fact that the fans loved it and women especially responded enthusiastically to it.[28]

This came at a time when promoters would not headline a show with a woman artist and when radio stations did not play two women artists' records in a row.[29] The conviction was that neither practice was smart from a money standpoint. But Kitty's record began to open a few doors.

Patsy Cline's career would open that door much further. Coming along in the late fifties and early sixties, Patsy was a blend of tough and tender. She could swear like a sailor, and tell you which side of hell was hottest and give clear directions for an early arrival there. Independent, brassy, hard as nails, she also had a vulnerable and outgoing heart. She reached out to people, especially to other women artists. Performers like Jan Howard, Dottie West, and Loretta Lynn express deep indebtedness to Patsy for her support and friendship in getting their careers going.

Patsy stood Nashville on its ear. She took it on, refusing to play out traditional women roles. In concert she was sheer electricity with an audience and countered all the stereotypes of what a female performer could do. Patsy Cline was the very incarnation of an extremely effective form of resistance that significantly affected the role of women in country music.

One of those she influenced was Loretta Lynn. No female artist does more to sing the lives of working women than this coal miner's daughter out of Butcher Holler. The characteristic Loretta increasingly personifies in her music is that of standing up to men. Just to read the lyrics of her songs from "Here in Topeka" to "Don't Come Home A'Drinkin' (With Lovin' on Your Mind)" to "The Pill" is to experience the increasing movement in defense of women, especially working women, in assertion with men.[30] No one in country music does this more effectively.

Many other women could be mentioned and more recent stars like Barbara Mandrell, Dolly Parton, Emmylou Harris, Reba McEntire, and others manifest significant resistance to the sexism in the industry and in the culture. Reba states that her goal is to "bond" with women, to be their friend, to sing their lives and their problems. As she says, "There's a lot of women out there who just want to have that three minutes of rebellion" in a country song.[31]

Resistance and especially everyday resistance, as in "three minutes of rebellion," have a long history in country music. It is an important dimension of a wider politics often missed in interpretations of country music and in approaches to working-class life. It is close to the very heart of white soul. We turn to this politics in the next chapter.

Chapter 8
Traditional Politics and Populist Anarchism

"Government is unrelated to my life."
—Betty Woods, homemaker and custodian

My grandmother, Jessie Boone Sartin, was a devoted Christian woman. My earliest memories of church are going with her to the Assembly of God where her brother-in-law preached. Long before anyone knew about the martial arts in the United States, my granny understood aikido. She would grab me by the wrist and hold my attention throughout the long services and my Uncle Ligon's forty-five-minute-plus sermons. I understood that I would do her bidding as long as she held onto my arm. Meanwhile she could sit there transfixed on the sermon and oblivious to my bored recalcitrance. I knew there was a God—only a supernatural power could be the source of such strength and endurance from such an otherwise gentle and unassuming soul—unless she got mad.

And she could get mad. My most memorable moment of her anger came when her son-in-law, my Uncle Lavelle, ran "The Barracks Club" in Brookhaven. It was one of those inexpensive places with about a dozen army surplus cots where working men could get a shower and a bunk for the night. It was also a place where my uncle sold bootleg whiskey. Brookhaven was a dry town, so my uncle made a pretty good living selling bonded whiskey and maybe a little white lightning out of the club. He paid off law enforcement people in order to stay in business.

During those years Brookhaven had a chief of police who will go here by the fictitious name of Bull Turnipseed. He was a big man, six feet two and about 240 pounds. He was an old football player and had a reputation for being rough. My uncle paid him $75 a week to buy him off, which was a whole lot of money back then. Still, the chief came by my uncle's place and demanded more money. When Lavelle refused, the chief slapped him. Not only did the chief have all that legal authority behind him, he outweighed my uncle a hundred pounds. Even so, without that badge my uncle would have evened the odds with a .38-caliber pistol for such occasions.

I was fortunate enough to be standing in my grandmother's living room when the phone call came, telling her of the chief's action. She didn't even pause. As soon as she hung up, she called the police station and, unfortunately for him, got the chief on the line.

"Chief Bull Turnipseed!" she shouted, her voice rising as she tried to corner her fear and then draw on her anger. Her tone took on a menacing twang that would strike terror in a carnivorous dinosaur. "Do you know who this is?" He did.

"You're goddamn right you do! This is Mrs. John Robert Sartin, and you better understand something, Chief Bull Turnipseed." When she was really angry she used full names, complete with titles.

"I don't approve of what my son-in-law does down there on front street, but I also don't approve of you being on the take either. But I'll tell you one thing and you better hear me. If Lavelle is violating the law, you take him to jail. But you better not hit him or anybody in my family ever again. Do you understand? If you do, I am going to bring my broom to town and I'm going to beat your ass up and down both sides of Main Street! You got that Chief Bull Turnipseed?"

So far as I know, he never said anything but "Yes, Ma'am."

That's the only instance of political action I ever knew my grandmother to take. She probably voted Democratic—at least everybody else did in those years—but she never had a political position so far as I knew. Her world was her family and the things that affected them. She probably would not have participated in a demonstration if her life depended on it. The government was always there, of course, but it just didn't have much to do with her affairs. That is, until Chief Bull got himself in "the line of fire." Most of the time she just avoided getting tangled up with the government. My grandmother would have agreed with Betty Woods at the beginning of this chapter: "Government is unrelated to my life." Such a politics is characteristic of many working people and well reflected in country music.

A Traditional Politics

Dorothy Horstman maintains that the commercial character of country music has kept it from being politically left or right, except in specific cases. It has been more middle-of-the-road. "Executives of recording companies have seldom been known for advanced social thinking; their success . . . has depended on their ability to predict public tastes more than to formulate them." In addition, while there have been individual artists who expressed views right or left, these have not been widely popular and not commercially successful.[1]

Horstman, however, goes on to say that even stronger reasons for the absence of such political views are "the enduring social values" of country music fans. She labels these as "individualist," meaning that "the rugged southern citizen has been a strong individualist, suspicious of governments and 'movements,' jealous of his privacy and freedoms."[2] She argues that the paternalism of the Old South even worked against class identities. Hence, Southerners saw the upper-status planters as individuals—more fortunate, perhaps "more deserving" than themselves—but not representative of a ruling class.

Moreover, Horstman suggests that Calvinist doctrines of personal sin and retribution led people to blame not the system but themselves. Further, much of Southern rage was aimed at the Yankees of the North and East. And, finally, deep

123

pride in the South itself and a solidarity that stands over against outsiders has long been in place and continues into the present.[3]

Horstman is onto something important here, but her label is not helpful. It is a mistake to see these things in individualistic terms, not because there is no individualist dimension, but because the individual in country music stands in a wider framework, one distorted by the use of such language.

A political continuum like right, middle, and left does not appear frequently not only because of commercial reasons, for example, but also because this continuum is not the basic framework operative in working-class politics. These people are more like my grandmother or dozens of other people, women and men, for whom government is unrelated to their lives, except, it seems, when it becomes intrusive.

The basic framework of such people is a more traditional one. The political continuum of right, middle, and left characterizes modernist political commitments that are not the operative commitments of most working people. Until one sees country fans and most country artists, certainly the ones who have embodied working-class lives, as operating from a more traditionalist base, then their politics will be missed. Actually Horstman senses this with her attention to suspicion of government and movements, and the jealousy of privacy and freedom.

I indicate above the contradiction between tradition and modernity and report Rebecca Klatch's helpful distinction between traditional commitments and conservative ones. In the remainder of this chapter I want to suggest a way of looking at country music as the expression of a politics informed by these discussions, a politics that is traditionalist and populist, but not basically modern in the sense of contemporary characterizations of political positions.

Populist Anarchism

A good way to approach this question is with the work of Merle Haggard. No one better represents working people than Haggard, unless it is Loretta Lynn. Haggard is perhaps most known for his song "Okie from Muskogee." This song typically gets labeled as a flag-waving, authoritarian, super-patriotic, reactionary song, and those who do not know his work well paint Haggard in these terms. It is a colossal mistake.[4]

First, look at the song. Haggard himself reports: "It's a funny song, a ridiculous song in some ways. It has so many different messages. It has messages that I didn't even know were there, and I wrote it."[5] The song makes it clear that things like marijuana, LSD, orgies, long shaggy hair, and beads and sandals are not popular in Muskogee. It promotes flag waving, holding hands, pitching woo, leather boots, respect for the college dean, and white lightning. Muskogee is a place where people do not burn draft cards, yet it says: "But we like living right and being free." Strictly speaking, it does not say anything about what others can or cannot do. Rather, it speaks to what people do in Muskogee. It is not, to be sure, a defense of the free individual, a modernist doctrine, but of a way of life. At this point it is not a right-wing conservatism but a traditionalism. It does defend being free, but this is in a context of living right as a way of life.

Even "The Fightin' Side of Me," which is a far more resistant song, has the language of "love it or leave it" and warns war protesters that they are "walkin' on the fightin' side" of Merle. It does have an important line: "I don't mind them switchin' sides and standin' up for things they believe in." This in itself is an astounding statement. What I see here is a belief that a person can do what they believe; they had just better be prepared to fight for it. It is not standing up for what they believe in that is the problem, but "runnin' down our country" and "runnin' down our way of life" while not changing sides.[6]

I personally do not side with the sentiments of these two songs, but the traditional stance can easily be read from the lyrics. I begin with the toughest songs in Merle's repertoire, because neither one of them is typical of his work. Even here a traditionalism, not a conservatism, is basically at work.

Bill Malone states that "Okie from Muskogee" cast Haggard "in the role of right-winger," and "over-shadowed his sensitive statements about working-class life."[7] His songs, like "Hungry Eyes," for example, contain sharp criticism of a world where his father and mother's hard work did not pay off because another class took all they could.[8]

James Ring Adams wrote in the Reagan years, during a revival of new traditionalists in the music. He states that "there's nothing in this cultural revival that should cheer the strategists of any political establishment." Instead, he argues that among those of "another America," you encounter "a populism distrustful of all political parties. . . . Hard core country fans have little use for any sort of social elite." Adams claims that the best way to discover the people of this America is to talk with country musicians who have significant rapport with their fans. Emphasizing the up-close relationship performers have with their audiences "at country fairs, dance halls and honky tonks," Adams points out that "Even the biggest names emphasize their plain-folks origins. Their personal histories show vividly the many varieties of traditionalism, and the singleness of its purpose."[9]

This is an important part of the picture, but another ingredient needs to be added. In discussing Merle Haggard's "complicated soul," Tony Scherman suggests that Haggard "hews to a sort of right-wing anarchism" and states that in his best songs rightly deserves the title "the poet of the common man." Scherman's important point misses the key component.[10]

It is not a right-wing, but a populist, anarchism, and this makes all the difference in the world. A conservative wants to do battle so that the individual is free to pursue rational economic activity. A liberal wants an individual who can make full use of civil liberties and human rights to enact free speech and to actualize self in the public and private sphere. But a populist anarchism of a traditional sort wants to be free from the institutional entrapments of a modern world. He or she wants to be left the hell alone. They do not trust the free individualism of the laissez-faire conservatives because they know it serves the rich, but neither do they support the freedoms and rights of the American Civil Liberties Union because they know basically it is the reserve of intellectuals and elites.

We miss this point because political thought in the United States has been so entrapped by the aftermath of eighteenth-century political thought, with its struggles over the free or mixed market, the role of the state in the economy, and the protection of individuals from both the big state and powerful economic concentrations. Think for but a moment about how much power you have—or think you have—even to engage in those kinds of discussions. Such conversation requires "position" and "education," some of it ephemeral indeed. I sometimes hear professionals talk about what "our policy" will be in Eastern Europe, as though "we" really will determine it.

A traditional populist anarchism is not political in a programmatic sense. Neither is it ideological in the sense of an explicit position on social policy. It is something more like a feeling or a way of being in the world. It has a quality of rebellion, a sharp sense of independence, and a spirit that warns: "Don't tread on me." Highly suspicious of control, it distrusts theory and theorists. For one thing, working people do not think in theories; and they are suspicious of anything that has "fine print." "Fancy talk" has an angle; it promotes somebody else's interests, and it is a source of control.

An objection to traditional populist anarchism is that working people are highly patriotic. While I can quibble about this as a stereotype—working people, for example, were less supportive of the Vietnam War than upper middle-class business and professional people—let me instead point to the relationship between patriotism and a deep distrust of government among working people. This patriotism is deeply rooted in a love of country, based in traditional values, while there is a profound suspicion of the nation-state as expressed in governmental control.[11] This basic stance of working people is more than consistent with a traditional populist anarchism. Notice how the talk among working people is about defending "our way of life." They are not nearly so interested in defending the interests of the nation-state.

127

Nevertheless, this kind of patriotism has been vulnerable to the tawdriest kind of idolatrous chauvinism. The basic challenge to this, however, needs to come from a position that drives a wedge between love of country and unwarranted obedience to the nation-state, affirming the former and generating deep suspicion about the latter.

Such efforts are not as distant as one might think. A populist anarchism will say "to hell with it, just leave me alone." This is happening on a large scale today and can best be seen in the large numbers of people in the bottom half of the class structure who do not vote. Quite frankly, it is a good question whether the interests of working people are better served by voting. The moderate shifts of elites and their power holdings may be affected by such demographic presence in the polls, but does it actually affect the lived lives of working people? Would a genuine liberal, for example, have really affected the loss of good-paying, high-benefits jobs in the United States or would it have been covered with better, more humane ideology?

It is arguable whether withdrawal from the political arena serves working people better than staying in it. It may be best for the elites, right and left, in the U.S. to get worried about the withdrawal of working people and begin to change their agendas. But conservatives, liberals, and left-wingers don't typically give a damn about working people. Such political "sophisticates" mainly want to use the working masses to achieve some vision these cosmopolitans have, which usually serves interests other than those who work. Listen to their language about "rednecks" in spite of the fact that research has consistently shown that most working people are more moderate about issues for which they are usually scored as authoritarian. Most privileged people in this country have about as much sophistication about working people as Dorothy Kilgallen did about country music in the sixties.

While I do not finally endorse the political withdrawal of working people in the U.S., hardly anything is more important in understanding working people than to grasp this traditional populist anarchism, and country music is as good a place as there is to see it at work. Hank Williams, Jr.'s "A

Country Boy Can Survive" is another good example, as is the work of Dwight Yoakam, who hit the country scene in the mid-eighties. His song about the highway out of Kentucky says: "They thought readin', rightin' / Rt. 23 / Would take them to the good life / That they had never seen / They didn't know that old highway / Could lead them to a world of misery."[12]

Among the best work on traditional life is that of Loretta Lynn and Dolly Parton. Loretta's "Coal Miner's Daughter" and her strong defense of working people throughout her career certainly illustrate the importance of traditional commitments. Dolly's "Coat of Many Colors" and many other songs also involve deep, positive valuations of tradition.

When one thinks about women and tradition one usually thinks of Tammy Wynette's "Stand By Your Man." This certainly reflects a traditional view, but it is not the whole picture. Traditional life is not now and has never really been about keeping together the nuclear family. Spousal relations are very important, but traditional life has been about sustaining extended family and communal relationships. These are more basic to coping and survival in traditional life ways. One often hears about how families stayed together during the Great Depression. Divorce statistics were relatively low, but desertion rates soared. People survived the Depression not so much through nuclear families but through extended familial and communal ties, often in spite of broken husband-wife relationships. Working-class women know this as well as anybody in the society.

Traditional practices endure even as they change. We are seeing such changes, as well as challenges, to traditional life in country music today. Some of it continues to hark back to the good old days as in Wynonna and Naomi Judd's "Grandpa (Tell Me 'Bout the Good Old Days)." But Mary Chapin Carpenter sings appreciatively about a town in Carolina that tells her plainly "I am not your destination / I am clinging to my ways / I am a town."[13] On the one hand, it defends the town, but on the other, the singer knows that the town cannot be for her. This sense of loss and the inability to recover the past and its traditions are also part of the music, and the contradiction between tradition and modernity continues to permeate it.

So far, I contend that the best reading of the politics of country music as it is used by working people is as a form of resistance and as a traditional populist anarchism. Not all country music and every working person take this stance; some clearly do not. Yet, it is the deepest current in the music that embodies working-class life. It is not the traditionalism of the turn of the century, but traditionalism itself changes. What we are seeing in our own time is a persistence of this form of life even as it takes new shapes. With this in mind we examine three other basic aspects of this traditional political formation.

Beating the System

Working people in the United States do not see any sharp change from what is going on. They anticipate no radical alteration in existing arrangements, at least that would serve their interests. The first thing, then, about a traditional populist anarchism is that you do not attempt to overthrow the system. It is far more typical to try to beat the system. Beating the system is a basic form of resistance. It is a way of asserting that the system does not have full control.

One example of this is Johnny Cash's "One Piece at a Time." This song tells the story of a man who goes from Kentucky to Detroit and begins a job putting wheels on Cadillacs. He gets the idea to take home with him an automotive part a day so that he can assemble his own Cadillac by the time he retires. He sneaks out small parts in his lunchbox, and the engine and other large components in his buddy's motor home. As one might expect he has trouble getting the parts from different model years to fit together, but with no little ingenuity he does it. For example, he has to drill new holes in the block so that engine parts from different models can be bolted together. "With a little help from an adapter kit / We had that engine runnin' like a song."

When he finally takes his wife for a spin to get the tags, he confesses that the courthouse people were not pleased because it took the whole staff to type up the title, and, when they did, it weighed sixty pounds! He is proud of the fact that it didn't cost him a dime and it's "the only one there is around."

This is truly a populist piece with the crafty use of "resources" like lunchboxes and mobile homes, and it displays the ingenuity and coping skills of working people in their capacity to get by and make it. In a nod to morality, he states that he "never considered myself a thief / But GM wouldn't miss just one little piece / Especially if I strung it out over several years."[14]

The humor and the fantastic lack of realism in the song should not be missed. Working people know it is impossible to put a Cadillac together in this way. To most working people this is a celebration of beating the system. It is the victory of ingenuity over official manufacturing standards and operating procedures. It is the capacity to make do with the miscellany of the system. And, not to be missed, notice what the song does to the bureaucracy at city hall. It requires the whole staff at no little inconvenience to type up the title, and in testimony to bureaucratic paper work—the bane of existence for working people—the damn thing weighs sixty pounds!

Rejection of the Official World

A second ingredient in a traditional populist anarchism involves the rejection of the dominant world. All that I say above is testimony to this claim. In country music we have a rejection of the discourse, affect, taste, etiquette, and propriety of the established upper class and elitist world. Country music challenges these with refusal, parody, mockery, protest, defiance, burlesque, and humor—corny and otherwise. Such populist tactics characterize the music and the lives of working people.

Closely related to the rejection of the established world is a deep suspicion of official truth. This is perhaps best seen in the distrust of government and the critique of bosses in working-class life and in country music. This is not hard to understand. Working people are subject to close supervision and their views are often not taken into account at work or by government.

The distrust of government is quite clear in Travis Tritt's rendition of "Lord Have Mercy on the Working Man." The song laments: "Uncle Sam's got his hands in my pockets / And he helps himself each time he needs a dime / Them politicians treat me like a mushroom / 'Cause they feed me bull and keep me blind."[15]

In Dolly's "9 to 5" there is the clear realization that work is for the sake of the boss's ambition and that she will not be served by her hard effort. They will use her but she will not get any credit for it. An intense animosity toward the bosses where "the foreman is a lowdown dog" and "the line boss is a fool" takes place in "Take This Job and Shove It." A similar animosity occurs in "Oney," but with a different twist. In this song about an overbearing boss, the singer is a worker who has stayed in shape and got stronger while Oney, the boss, has got soft in his supervisory role. When the worker retires he is going to let Oney feel the power of his fists. The song ends with his retirement and calling the boss outside.[16]

Systemic Issues, Heartache, and Humor

The third form that a populist traditional approach takes is usually not "ideological." What I mean by this is not that there are no interests served by traditionalist forms, but that issues are handled differently. Country will not typically approach a social or political issue head-on. Rather, it will sing about the heartaches accompanying the issue and address the feelings involved. Another way to address these issues is through humor and upbeat music. On the one hand, it will typically put a face on such problems and give them a human and personal form or, on the other, provide a humorous but very clear exposure of the problem.

In the first case, Dorothy Horstman points out the deep ambivalence that country music takes to war. She points out that the attitude "is a more personal one, more concerned with its effects than its causes."[17] The stereotype of country music as jingoist and superpatriotic is not true. While such songs exist, far more characteristic are the stories of the pain, separation, loss, and tragedy of war, with the most prominent theme being that of the loss of a loved one. Even in the sixties when country music produced a number of superpatriotic songs, Horstman reports that "Southerners . . . stood not so much in favor of the war in Southeast Asia as opposed to the war protesters, whom they considered unpatriotic."[18] It is worth remembering that when war is fought, it will be the working people and racial and ethnic minorities who will do most of the fighting and dying. Perhaps this reality has something to do with the ambivalence of country music to war.

Other issues are also dealt with in terms of the heartaches and personal discontent attending them and not an analysis of the issue as such. Illustrations of these abound in the music. For example, issues of class are dealt with in terms of such discontent in "Old Five and Dimers (Like Me)"[19] or in "Po' Folks."[20] Issues of racism are approached with songs like "Skip a Rope"[21] or, as we have seen, "I Want to See the Parade."

This approach to social and political issues from a standpoint of personal pathos that puts a human face on systemic suffering and injustice is an important ingredient in traditional and populist practices. It will be central to any efforts for social change as it relates to working people, as we will see in the last chapter.

In the second case, country music will approach a lot of issues with humor and with upbeat tunes. This is a kind of indirection, but a very important one. I think of the song "Put Another Log on the Fire." The lyrics are a scalding critique of male supremacy in which the singer gives his wife a continual list of things to do such as iron, cook, chop wood, and so on, while he apparently is doing nothing at all except being a "no good, good ole boy." He then tells the woman to "put another log on the fire" and give some reason, some explanation for why she is leaving him. It is a powerful lyric, and I have seen it used very effectively with working people. Because it is country and funny and done with an upbeat tune, it enables an otherwise resistant group to hear its message.[22]

In sum, a profound stream of resistance runs through country music. It rejects dominant language, affect, taste, etiquette, and aesthetics. That this is itself a politics is often missed by observers of country music, and especially by critics of mass culture. It is an everyday resistance, one that expresses itself in the identities, pleasures, and meanings of the music. It is a resistance that sets up "a place apart," a site of protest and lament. The history of women in country music is an important instance of this politics of resistance. It is a movement within the music and one growing in strength even as it encounters the ebb and flow of the battle of the sexes.

Implicit in this resistance is a traditional populist anarchism that cannot be reduced to the political continuum of conservative/moderate/liberal in the United States. It is not ideologically formed as in a position or platform, but is expressed in an independence from the dominant institutions of the society. The attempt is not to overthrow the system but to beat it. It rejects the authoritative world of the establishment and deeply distrusts official truth. It is not a discursive analysis of social and political issues but rather it puts a human face on them and sings the heartache and pathos of working-class life.

This politics of resistance and populist anarchism offers a host of implications for response by the church and its ministry, especially for those who take indigenous approaches to change seriously. We examine these questions in the next chapter.

PART IV

The Implications for the Church

Chapter 9
The Church as a Community of Resistance

I worked my way through college in an oil field outside my hometown. I was a roustabout, meaning I did not work on a drilling rig, but laid pipeline, did maintenance and repair, and fought the inroads of grass and weeds around oil tanks and well locations. Everyone there knew that I was "going into the ministry." It was a ripe topic for mockery and derision on those days when the work was long and hard, and the end of it in the distance beyond several days of nasty, exhausting labor.

One of the men in the group, whom I will call "Jukes," had a kind of love/hate relationship with me. He was fascinated not so much with me personally as with the fact that I was going into the ministry. It seemed never far from his mind, especially when I had all I could do just to keep swinging a pick or a sledgehammer or throwing pipe on a truck. I believe now that it was one of the ways Jukes managed to stay out there and do the kind of work that sometimes drained your very soul.

Shortly after I began work in the field, we were laying a three-inch pipeline in a ditch with a foot of water in it. We were slipping and sliding around trying to match up the threads of joints of pipe that weighed about 250 pounds apiece. None of us was in a good mood. Covered with mud and knowing we would not finish laying the line until late the next day, we were two hours from lunch and nearly six hours from quitting time. I'm standing in water over my boots and not a little overmatched by my end of a pipe that seemed dedicated to throwing me on my butt in the slick bottom of that ditch. While wondering whether I really wanted to go to college this badly, Jukes starts in:

"Soooo, you think you got the call to go into the ministry." His sarcasm had a whiny, nasal, scathing quality that I can still hear.

"Yeah, I . . . think . . . so," I said tentatively. To be honest I felt "driven" to go into the ministry. I did not like the idea at all. I held in my mind just about every stereotype about ministry you can imagine. I ran from this strange urgency for three years, and did not find peace until I finally made the move. But I was still uncomfortable with the whole idea. To me most ministers were glad-handing "preachers" who talked funny in conversation and even stranger when they preached. They were always too "happy" and too "glad to see you." But worse than that, I was in no mood to think about the ministry while standing in the middle of that damn ditch.

"Shit!" said Jukes, "you ain't got no call to go into the ministry. You woke up one morning with a hard-on and the taste of chicken in your mouth and *thought* you had the call to preach!"

Bernell Birch, ever my defender in these moments, stepped in and an argument ensued that made the two hours before lunch go a lot faster. It was not lost on me that Jukes would always do something like that when the work was the worst.

But I never forgot the comment. He held ministry in deep suspicion as a place where men—in those days—pursued their erotic wonts of sexual desire and a full belly. It was no place of dedication and service, but the opportunity to cover with the palaver of pious language the egoistic aims of self-serving manipulation. While his fire was aimed at me, it became clear that Jukes held deep resentment toward the church and its ministry. His summation of my call was only one blast from a much larger broadside in a full-scale assault on institutional religion.

Yet, he spoke on no few occasions about his own "born again" conversion and how powerful it was. While he did not go to church, he "knew the Lord." The importance of his "being saved" seemed commensurate with his distrust of the church. I remember once when he came to tears while talking about his relationship to God, an embarrassment he quickly covered, and which he never let me see again.

Things of the spirit both in working-class life and in country music manifest this same contradiction. A sense that the church and authentic faith do not go hand in hand appears frequently in country music when things religious are in view. A common theme is expressed in one song: "I don't believe that heaven waits for only those who congregate." [1]

The Contradiction of Institutional Religion and White Soul Spirituality

Sometimes this contradiction can be almost as testy as that of Jukes. In "The Outlaw's Prayer" Johnny Paycheck sings about a country singer who has just "worked a big package show in Ft. Worth Saturday night" and on Sunday is rejected at a church because of his "big black hat, those jeans, that beard, and long hair."[2] After being refused entrance at "a big church on the corner of the square," the singer kneels down in front of the church and prays. He observes the hypocrisy of those now at prayer, who were dancing, drinking beer, and screaming "sing 'Shove It'" at his show last night. The song notes that one stained glass window from the church could feed a wino in the alley "bent over in tears" and his family for years. Realizing that neither Jesus nor John the Baptist with scandals, beard, and long hair could attend the church, the song states that when God takes everyone "To love forever in heaven with You / I'd sure hate to be in this crowd." He nails the point about the institutional church with the lines "So if this is what religion is, a big car and a suit and tie / Then I might as well forget it 'cause I can't qualify."

If anything, this song is a compilation of themes in country music about the church and authentic spirituality. First, the class issues can hardly be missed. It is a "big church on the corner of the square," it has expensive stained glass windows, and the people have big cars and wear suits and ties. The singer then admits that he "can't qualify." It's pretty clear that he does not want to be with this crowd even in heaven. Second, the rejection is just as clear. He is thrown out of a church. In protest he kneels outside, outside the realm of institutional religion. Third, he notes that the church is not meeting the needs of the poor, of the wino and his family. But, finally, his faith in God remains strong if one can believe the sincerity of his prayer.

One should also not miss the hypocrisy and arrogance in the song itself. It does not raise the question about how much the wino and his family could be helped by the proceeds of "a big package show in Ft. Worth," and no evidence is forthcoming that the singer does anything himself to aid the wino. The fire is so sharply directed at the church that there is no questioning or confession of the outlaw's failure to address the very issues for which he rips the church. Instances do exist when country songs take hold of the responsibilities of discipleship, but this is not one of them.

This separation of institutional religion and authentic faith permeates much of country music's depiction of spirituality. As with so many things about the music, Hank Williams embodied this characteristic as well. Hank was uninterested "in formal religion" and yet was deeply religious, at least in a sense. He talked about it a great deal, held deep feelings about it, took strong exception to using the Lord's name in vain (though he did), and wrote a significant proportion of his songs on religious themes.[3]

Saturday Night and Sunday Morning

Another aspect of Hank's life manifested this struggle over spirituality. Chet Flippo, one of his biographers, says that Hank "never really got it straight in his mind whether he was writing for Saturday night . . . or . . . for Sunday morning." He wanted the festivity of a honky-tonk Saturday night, but he also wanted the forgiveness and innocence of Sunday morning.[4]

The contradiction between institutional religion and heartfelt spirituality may be experienced in other parts of this culture but it is a powerful incongruity in country and deeply rooted in class inequalities.[5]

At least two other themes need explicit treatment here. First, one should not miss the deep contradiction of such a disparity between a people so connected to traditional life and yet so alienated from an institution like the church. Surely this says something about the church's relationship to the official world and to official truth. The rejection of the church in working-class life and in country music is part and parcel of a populist resistance that rejects the established order. The church, especially "fancy preaching" and a "fancy church"— as Tom T. Hall calls them—is caught in the profound fusions and oppositions of working-class life.[6] A church that is insensitive to its entrapment in such larger systemic social constructions simply will miss the powers at work to destroy or at least diminish its capacity for mission and ministry.

I do not mean to suggest that the church holds no responsibility for this resistance, as I shall suggest in more detail below, but an important aspect of the contradictions of working life and country music will be missed if the place of religion, spirituality, and the church is not seen as basic to the broader range of contradictions examined earlier.

Second, I want to underscore the contradiction between the festivity of Saturday night and the innocence of Sunday morning. David Sanjek points to the coexistence of hedonism and religiosity in Southern culture.[7] I am not sure this can be restricted to the South because it is deeply writ in working-class life, especially in traditional order, on the one hand, and in festivity and the wild side of life, on the other. This contradiction dogs working-class life. It is always there.

As I have tried to indicate, tradition brings order and safety from the chaos of life in the draining hazards of inequality. But the tradition brings control as well. It bears the restraints of survival and coping. It is often a hard, straight and narrow world. And the churches that have, in the main, served the working class in the past have been the churches of the true believers with a heavy conventional morality and a God of law and control. If they exploded in celebration at worship, they nevertheless preached the heavy duty of a narrow morality. This worked for some, but for others the control was stifling, too much like the rest of life. The hedonism, the honkytonk, the Saturday night, the carousing, the drinking, and the rowdy and loud celebration not only break traditional and institutional controls, they also use festivity as a form of resistance and "a place apart" to get out of the ordinariness of too much numbing work and too much unrelieved struggle with the rest of life.

In this context the church becomes one of the focal points of large scale and deeply negative resistance. It is a resistance difficult to overcome. Yet, one of the most crucial challenges before the church is to get past such resistance and to be in community with working people. When confronted with the wild side of life, the church often sees this too much in moralistic terms. As a result this view reduces a much larger scale of human issues to a narrow pattern of moral concern.

Biblically, it is the equivalent of straining at a gnat and swallowing a camel. The church gets overwrought about drinking and dancing and carrying on at the honky-tonk, and misses the politics of festivity and resistance against the dominant order. The church gets uptight about "bad language" but fails to see how and why such language is a protest of the dominant discourse. I never cease to be amazed by pastors who can criticize the language, the booze, and the honky-tonk, but never question the loss of real income and benefits, and then spiritualize everything the Bible says about the poor and the oppressed.

Such clergy are tools of the dominant order and serve the principalities and powers. The stories about Jesus teach us that one does not have to be complacent about destructive patterns in drinking and living on the wild side of life in order to stand with working people. It will, however, require a morality that begins in deep empathy with their worlds of pain and with appreciation for traditional tactics and populist anarchism.

The Church's Captivity to Class

The church, of course, is in deep captivity to class. This comment is not meant to bash the church. So far as I can tell it is no worse than other major institutions. The pain of the church's captivity is magnified in that it is an institution that could be so different. It does not have to be so entrapped. The church has more access than perhaps any other institution to the working people of this country. Moreover, many working people are vital members of churches, but these are churches too often given to the strategies of control, that is, to containing working lives in the patterns of respectability and/or "true belief." In such churches no major alternatives to the discontinuities of class existence and the dominant order are offered. As a result, many working people know in their bones that the church is no different, and that there is no real reason to be there.

The beginning of ministry is a sustained attack on the captivity of class. In the light of our study of country music as the embodiment of working life, three dimensions of this captivity need attention before turning to other directions for ministry. The first captivity is a conspiracy of taste. The captivity of the church to the aesthetic tastes of a professional and managerial class is pervasive. This results partly from the ethos of the dominant order, partly from the influence of an educated clergy, and partly from the makeup of most lay leadership, among other factors that could be named. In some churches this takes the form of a classical music program that is imposed by professional musicians who see their vocation in life to be that of "raising" the musical tastes of a local church. Where classical music is the soul music of a congregation, then Bach, Beethoven, Mozart, and Brahms are more than appropriate. When the soul music, however, is Hank, Kitty, George, Patsy, Merle, Loretta, Garth, and Dolly, then the external imposition of classical music is an abomination and brings stench to the nostrils of God. We must stop this violation of soul.

The second captivity is an imperialism of language. In 1492 Antonio de Nebrija observed in the introduction of his *Grammatica* that language has always been the partner *(compañera)* of empire. When the Bishop of Avila, speaking for the author, presented the volume to Queen Isabella, she asked the utilitarian question, "What is it for?" The Bishop answered "Your

Majesty, language is the first instrument of empire."[8] Linguistic colonialism has a long history, preceding even the fifteenth century. It is alive and well today.

The church's complicity in linguistic colonialism can be illustrated in three ways. First, in its captivity to the professional middle class it uses the highly differentiated conceptual discourse of the university trained. This is not the language of working people, which is far more concrete and situational. Here is where listening to country music can help one keep talk "closer to the ground." Second, middle-class language does a great deal of analysis of subjectivity and interiority. Working people tend instead, as we have seen, to show feelings rather than explore them. Third, the very use of proper language and the institutionalization of established linguistic standards sets up the church as a representative of the dominant order. In doing so it defines itself as the church of middle-class people and becomes the target of working-class resistance and refusal.

I am, indeed, suggesting that the church needs to let its linguistic hair down, to become much more adept at the linguistic practices of working people. Even so I must confess some despair about the church's superpious hypersensitivity to certain language, especially four-letter words. While I do believe that there are evil words, words nevertheless derive their meaning from how they are used, that is, the practices in which they are embedded and the worlds they assist in constructing. Some words are embedded in destructive and demeaning practices. I think of racist, sexist, and classist slurs, for example. Four-letter words can also be embedded in violative practices.

At the same time Bourdieu points out that "the refusal of the dominant code, which is often associated with rejection of the censorship that propriety imposes, particularly on the tabooed body, and with the outspokenness whose daring is less innocent than it seems since in reducing humanity to its common nature—belly, bum, bollocks, grub, guts and shit—it tends to turn the social world upside down, arse over head."[9]

I am not suggesting that the church begin to shout four-letter words during worship or develop religious signs that utilize the middle index finger. It will help, however, if the church begins to recognize the role of language in resistance and look past its moralisms to the practices in which these words are embedded. One does not need to believe that all the primal Anglo-Saxon words are used as revolutionary acts of resistance in order to see that working people tell us things in these practices.

A third class captivity of the church is the imposition of practices that are external to working people's lives. I think here especially of the church's use of the highly rationalized organizational procedures of corporate America. Executives are seized by a never-ending parade of practices, such as management by objectives, strategic planning, quality management, and visioning, to name but a few.

Let me overstate it. The church would be far better off in terms of indigenous ministry with working people if it utilized traditional tribal practices rather than the organizational technology of the corporations. In saying this, it is certainly not my intent to demean tribal life or working people. But the practices used by the church need to be far more traditional than modern, more folk than associational, more populist than elitist, and less into control and more into a working-class expressivism.

My conviction here is not that some romantic, nativist harmony issues out of working-class expressivity. It is not necessary to romanticize working-class people or to see some unwavering functional efficiency in their practices to recognize that they have endured and know how to get things done. They know how to survive, to cope, to hunker down, to live life. They have pragmatic approaches to things. The problem with imposed practices is that, on the one hand, they make working people feel alien—in the church of the carpenter, for Christ's sake!—and, on the other, they find themselves in resistance to the church because it is not "our church." It sets up one hell of a contradiction. The class captivity in the church is such that practices are imposed on the congregation that working people are already in resistance to in the larger society.

The church does not need to show working-class people

how to do things; they already know that. The church needs to demonstrate that it is "their" place and not a promotional come-on for the dominant order. Moreover, when the church is into control strategies—read this as "participative procedures to give people ownership while co-opting them into agendas and interests that are not theirs"—it is quite simply part of the problem, not the solution.

These three forms of captivity only touch the surface. Perhaps, however, they illustrate something of the entrapment of the church and the necessity for change. Let me say, too, that I am not addressing only establishment churches here. My sisters and brothers in denominations like the Church of the Nazarene, the Assemblies of God, and some of the Pentecostal churches, among others, are presently riding an upwardly mobile, lower middle-class constituency hot-breathed for success. You can already see the gleam of class legitimacy across their countenances. It is no better, or worse, than the smile of class satisfaction on the complacent faces of the dying old-liners.

Engaging the Contradictions

If awareness of class captivity and a rejection of its bondage is a first step in a ministry of pitching tent, then the engagement of the contradictions of working-class life is second. Here country music is a major resource because nothing in popular culture embodies the contradictions of working-class life so well. More than that, it captures the "idiom" of working-class expression in delineating them. It speaks their language with the right "accent." One would hardly attempt ministry with a Hispanic community without learning Spanish; and for many white working people, country is their "first language."

About ten years ago I was invited to do a "seminar" on working people and country music at a local church. The pastor told me that they would have the best country band in their area to assist in the worship and other parts of the program as I wished. When I met the band, they were obviously quite nervous. The bandleader admitted that "we're Christians, but we ain't been to church a lot lately and we ain't never been invited to play in one!"

When they began, they played very tentatively and stayed with gospel tunes, not very good ones at that. It was not working. Our effort was going down the drain. During a break the pastor and I put our heads together with the band. A very sagacious man, the pastor said,

"Hey, guys, why aren't you playing your usual stuff?"

"We're in church!" explained the leader.

"Well, look, guys, we do things a little different at this church. You see, we think the best religious music in country is the stuff that's not the sacred songs," the pastor gently stated.

It took a few minutes to assure them that he meant it, but when he said he wanted them to play "Help Me Make It Through the Night," they looked at him strangely and then reluctantly agreed to do so after he told them how important it was spiritually. As they began to get into the song and saw the response of the people to it, they "got going." Their whole manner changed and the atmosphere of the room suddenly shifted from awkward tentative struggle to celebrative festivity. As the workshop moved through issues of working people's lives and the way the music engages them, it was a delight just to watch their response. Things were named that they later said they "felt" but "had never put into words."

Few things have spoken to me so powerfully about the separation between the lives of working people and what so many of them see as the church. Each of those band members loved "Help Me Make It Through the Night." One of them said "it kinda talks about me." Yet, they saw no relation between the song and the church. It was downright painful for me to see how much they enjoyed playing and singing it in church. It simply never dawned on them that the issues in that song were something the church would care about, and yet, if we can trust the one guy's comment, "it kinda talks about me."

Country music gives the opportunity to talk about working-class life and to name the contradictions of their world. These contradictions, however, not only need to be named but

147

also engaged, and this engagement will shift on the basis of the kind of contradiction it is. For example, in the contradiction between tradition and modernity the struggle is usually over the roots and identity of the former and the dislocation and alienation of the latter, but it can also be, as seen above, between entrapment in the local community and the yearning to move beyond it. In the first case the church's job is to embody the life of working people and to become a place for identity and rootage. In the latter, the church is the place where people find ways out of a rigid location to help people find the new place where they are called to be.

In the contradictions around racism and sexism, the supremacist racial practices of discrimination and exclusion are countered with indigenous practices for addressing social issues. I think especially here again of the resources of country music. The ability of the music to put an issue in a story, to put human faces on the violations of racism and sexism, to display the heartache caused by a systemic evil, to use humor to approach a controversy as country does so well, and to employ upbeat music to deal with sensitive questions: these are but a few of the ways the music can address these kinds of contradictions.

Moreover, when a working-class congregation can trust that its own life ways are understood, respected, and cared for, much resistance to dealing with such issues will be relieved. When the approach to issues is an indigenous one, the change will not be so alien and those who work for it are much more likely to be "us" rather than "them."

In the case of the contradiction around romantic love, the music can lay out the salience of the question and address the role of economic factors in domestic turbulence. But it is more than consciousness raising. It means a congregational life alert to financial struggles by families and the need for specific care and support during times of crisis. Naming the threat to love posed by financial hardship and pulling a community of faith around households in trouble is a basic form of ministry that engages the contradictions. Further, church support groups that are made up of people who have lost their jobs and that give them opportunity to deal with these issues with people "in the same boat" have proved to be very effective and life-saving for some people.

The contradiction of defiance and submission needs attention as well. This contradiction can be discussed as we deal with resistance.

Dealing with Resistance

Presently it is difficult to convey adequately the depth of resistance in working life. This resistance is felt througout the American population, expressed in dissatisfaction toward leaders of any dominant party. The rejection of institutional authority, the opposition to programs handed down from above or developed in one setting to be applied in another, the resentment of experts, the withdrawal from politics and voting, and the distrust of established institutions all speak to a deepening chasm rifting through American life. Working-class resistance is at the core of this and is no easy problem to deal with. It runs deep. Moreover, the church has a kind of "Constantinian" problem. The church is associated with the "official world" and with "official truth." That is, we are the enemy.

I know of no way to break through such resistance apart from joining it, or in the language of the Gospel of John, to pitch tent with it. In the instances where I know of this happening, the response is electric. In the 1980s when Iowa was reeling from the impact of the farm crisis and family farms were being lost, Rueben Job was the United Methodist bishop of that state. My friend Bill Cotton was a district superintendent in south central Iowa, an area experiencing some of the worst of the crisis. Bishop Job attended Cotton's district meeting. When he stood to address the meeting, he simply said:

"Before we do anything else let me just say that we will close no churches in this district because you can't pay the bills. You just be faithful and be the church. We'd rather have you than your money."

Cotton reports that from then on the churches paid out their bills in full, and Cotton's district led all the others in paying denominational askings. Needless to say no churches were closed. In that incident Job became not *the* bishop, but *our* bishop.

Something very important is at work here and it is reflected in country music. I cannot find anywhere in country music—though there surely must be some places—where the church is expected to do anything other than what it ought to do: to worship genuinely, to pray authentically, to be faithful to the gospel, to be compassionate about the poor, to care about the sick, the heartbroken, the lonely, the discouraged, the bereaved, the dead, the lost, the orphan, the widow, the friendless, the homeless, and so on. The critique from country music is rather about the church's failure to be like Jesus, to close off people who need it, to serve the rich and neglect the poor and needy, and to be high-handed and hypocritical. It is not necessary for the church to violate its mission when it joins the resistance of working people. Indeed, it opens the possibility of doing its work.

In this regard, the more basic problem for country music is its failure to go far enough in its expectations of the church. It does not address itself sufficiently to questions of peace and justice. While it does offer indigenous ways to approach these questions, it seldom takes on the systemic issues directly and hence does not expect the church to do so.[10]

What would it mean for the church to join the resistance? For churches accommodated to professional and managerial middle-class lifestyles yet serving working people, it will mean something like a self-emptying. It consists of taking the form of working-class life. In worship it will be a move from literate discourse to oral practices that minimize the reading of texts and maximize the use of stories and proverbs. It involves the use of the soul music of working people rather than the imposed canons of elitist taste, and no little of it from the work of country. It entails Christian education that will look more like apprenticeship in learning the meaning of Christian mission and less like a classroom, that is, the work of the church is learned by doing it. It requires that programming will be done not through the efficiencies of rationalized organizational practices, but through the power of gathering—more like Pentecost and less like the Pentagon. It will take its cues from the annual turkey supper and not the Harvard Business School. It means that the life of the congregation will be celebrated not only in worship, but in festivities, in jubilees that do indeed mock and dethrone the principalities and powers of the dominant order.

Further, the practices of resistance will find their deserved theological legitimation. The work of such a church is a divestment of status in the name of a holy *kenosis*, where the effort, indeed, is to let the same mind be in us that was in Christ Jesus, who not only pitches tent with us, but also takes the form of a working person in our midst. These are but a few of the moves to be made, but suggest something of the direction needed.

Populist Anarchism

Pitching tent and joining the resistance will involve the church in a venture of populist anarchism. I hope it is clear that by anarchism I do not mean some desperate and crazed individual souls running around with bombs in their hands or with vans full of fertilizer. By the term populist anarchism I am trying to convey the level of resentment and resistance working people have to the larger system that is imposing its patterns upon them. It is a defiance of city hall, the rich, the hierarchies, the experts, the bosses—the official world. It is an independence that stresses freedom, but this is not the free individual of a conservatism that wants to be unfettered in the pursuit of self-interest and economic enterprise or of a liberalism that wants to pursue achievement and self-fulfillment. The independent freedom of working-class anarchism seeks emancipation from the control of established, dominant institutions and latitude for another way of life. These are very different things. The first two are modern and establishment; the latter is traditional and populist.

What would it look like for the church to pitch tent with a populist anarchism? Before moving into this question, let me say that what I suggest here will be too abstract because we do not at present have the critical mass of working-class people participating in the kind of church I propose. Hence, we do not have the range of practices in place to learn from and to build on. As long as this is kept in mind I feel more able to dream possibilities so long as we remember the need for these things to be developed in the practices of parish life. We turn to these matters in the next chapter.

Chapter 10
The "Trashy" Church

Quentin Bennett is a pastor in north central Kansas. Late one Friday afternoon he was working in his study at the church, with country music playing on the radio, when someone knocked at the door. Answering it, Quentin found a teenager that he knew from the youth group of the church. As he came in he gave Quentin a high sign that it was good music he heard. The young man had had some real trouble lately. Several weeks earlier he had lost a job, one that he needed very much because he was not from a well-to-do family. About a week after that the young woman he was in love with broke off the relationship. About that same time he went to the high school basketball game in his hometown and was jumped on by a local "tough" and decked.

He told Quentin the basic outlines of the story, that it "hurt like hell," that he had considered suicide but couldn't go through with it. Even as they talked, however, Quenton knew that he was not connecting with him. The teen spoke without showing emotion; and Quentin was giving it his "Clinical Pastoral Education" best with nods and "uh-huhs," but Quentin knew they were not speaking the same language.

Soon the young man got up and began to pace the floor, saying that it was just too painful to talk about. Knowing that he was losing him, Quentin became anxious. The last thing he wanted was for this teen to walk out the door without "feeling" some sense of grace and hope. As Quentin said "I wanted to make sure he had something that would help him 'make it through the night.' "

"Do you see any light at the end of the tunnel?" Quentin asked.

"I guess, but I'm never sure."

In desperation, and trying to "connect," Quentin responded, "You mean its like that [country] song 'I see the light at the end of the tunnel, but I sure hope it's not a train.'"

With that the teen stopped dead in his tracks, shot around to look at Quentin but with his face beaming in recognition that someone had finally understood. He almost shouted: "Exactly! That's exactly what it's been like with her. Every time I think things are 'OK,' the light at the end of the tunnel turns out to be another freight train!"

Quentin is a quick study and came back quickly: "You know, when I go through tough times like this, I always think of Hank Williams's song, 'I'm So Lonesome I Could Cry.'"

"Oh, yeah," the teen responded, almost shouting, "that song says more about what I feel than words could ever say!"

Quentin, now warming to the opportunity, reached out with, "Man, you need to understand 'you got friends in low places.'"

"I know it, and I would rather 'have a bottle in front of me than a frontal lobotomy,'" he came back, obviously now getting into it.

But with that comment Quentin sensed that he needed to introduce a bit of theology at this point. He offered Mike Reid's song: "You need to 'walk on faith.'"

"Yeah, I know, I'm 'standing knee deep in a river and dying of thirst.'"

"You need to 'let go of the stone.'"

"But 'sometimes you're the windshield and sometimes you're the bug!'" the young man countered with an authority that transcended his years.

Quentin asked him if he could resist attempting to call her.

"I'm just gonna say to her: 'If your phone doesn't ring, baby, it's me.'"

"What if she gets in touch with you?"

"I'm just gonna give her 'a quarter and tell her to call someone who cares.'"

One-liners out of country songs went on like this for over

an hour. After a session of quotations that obviously named the young man's pain and provided him the next steps for coping with the situation, Quentin asked him if he would like to pray. He would. After the prayer he walked out the door, turned, and offered one last line, "Quentin, I know why 'Bubba shot the jukebox.'" With that, he laughed and walked away.

I argue in chapter 9 that the task of the church is to pitch tent with the indigenous practices of a people. Quentin embodies this kind of ministry in the session with the young man. By such a suggestion I do not mean, nor would Quentin, that the church should simply accommodate itself to whatever is going on in working people's lives. Pitching tent is not an automatic taking up of any practice that happens to be indigenous, no matter what it is.

Pitching Tent and Changing the Story

I do not, however, see indigenization as theologically neutral or bereft of Christian import. When Jesus pitches tent in the world, this is not simply a move of the Christ into the world so that a new ingredient is now part of the mix. That God pitches tent with us, that God makes habitation with us is an entirely new way of understanding the story of the world. Christ does not merely enter the story of the world; the story of the world is changed by his Incarnation. With his coming the story of the world becomes part of God's story. This does not mean that everything done in the world is God's will or that all practice is to be accepted. It means that the world, even with its sin and death, its principalities and powers, its exploitation, war, and want are now a part of a history whose destiny is in God.

In the meanwhile, a redemptive current is turned loose in history. In the Gospel of John we learn that after Jesus pitches tent with the world, performs his ministry, suffers death and rises, a Comforter will come and will now be active in the world doing the work of Christ. In this sense once the world's story is seen as part of God's story, everything changes.

155

From this point on a basic part of the mission of the church is to discern the work of the Spirit in the world. It is to search in everyday practices for the action of the Spirit. The church can then move with confidence that people of faith are not called anywhere, do not go anywhere, do not find themselves in any place where God in the Spirit has not already preceded them. I see in Quentin's act of ministry a discernment of the work of the Spirit and a vital and perceptive response to that work.

This is not to suggest that the church has no distinctive practices authentic to its own life. The church is called to engage the world with practices of its own: worship, baptism, Eucharist, catechesis, hospitality to strangers, the option for the poor, the commitment to the outcast, the witness to the good news, the bearing of joy and suffering within the community of faith, and the practices of justice and peace. All these are central to the identity and work of the church.

At the same time, I believe that working-class life is a location of the redemptive work of the Spirit. As one dimension of this the work of the Spirit is to be seen in the "soul music" of working people. Again, this is not a wholesale identification of the work of the Spirit with working-class life or with country music, but rather that the work of the Spirit is to be found in the midst of such practices.

Resistance and the Spirit

I am especially impressed by the practices of resistance found in both working-class life and country music as locales where the salvific work of the Spirit can be found. In the challenge to the supremacist claims of the dominant order in taste, etiquette, affect, and politics we have redemptive work afoot.

Furthermore, the practices of resistance are a key point for the work of the church in pitching tent. It is difficult to exaggerate the importance of resistance in the church's ministry. For one thing, the church is so often a representative of the "official world" and a target of working-class resistance itself. If the church does not join working-class resistance, it is difficult to see how it can pitch tent with the people themselves. Second, this resistance is a point of energy and momentum for addressing systemic issues that presently grind up many working-class lives. Third, resistance is a major resource for standing against accommodation to the status quo. It is crucial to counter the compromise and compliance that are inevitably a part of living in the world. No one escapes such acquiescence and it ever places limits on Christian existence, but resistance is crucial to the struggle against this accommodation.

The Trashy Church

In 1 Corinthians, Paul says to the church at Corinth that not many of them "were wise by human standards, not many were powerful, not many were of noble birth. But God chose what is foolish in the world to shame the wise; God chose what is weak in the world to shame the strong; God chose what is low and despised in the world, things that are not, to reduce to nothing things that are, so that no one might boast in the presence of God" (1:26-29). In a contemporary idiom God chose the "trashy" people and formed "the trashy church."

It is not my intention to be demeaning to working people by choosing this metaphor for the working-class church, but rather to take the metaphor and turn it into a highly positive and biblically informed metaphor. It is my intention to counter the supremacist claims of the dominant culture, to challenge the valuations "in vogue," to counter the "cultivated charm," the "sophisticated wit," and the "highbrow refinement" that legitimate social inequality. The trashy church engages the contradictions of working-class life, joins the resistance of laboring people, and takes up a politics of populist anarchism.

In suggesting that the trashy church adopt this stance, however, I am not proposing that the church simply adopt every expression of working-class life. I am also not suggesting that the church has nothing distinctive of its own to bring to such an enterprise. Here is a point where the church can offer a range of resources that not only are of major value to such a politics, but also are forms of faithful life and witness. The following five are distinctive contributions.[1]

First, the church can place such a politics in the framework of the Christian story. The challenge that Christ delivers to the principalities and powers, and the promise of victory over them as the destiny of the world provide the narrative of a different reality, in which a politics of resistance and populist anarchism gains ultimate importance and legitimation. John Masefield once said that "history is one damned thing after another."[2] The Christian faith offers a very different story of the world that intensifies the importance and meaning of resistance and proclaims its ultimate victory.

When the Word pitches tent with the people of Jesus' time, it is not simply adding a touch of God to the world. The Incarnation does not merely add an event from God to human life. Rather, it reveals that the world's story is God's story. Our story takes place in a much larger story. The fundamental politics of the church is to live out the implications of being the people of God in this story. To do so is to be a strange people and to live a story in no little tension with the powers that be. That is, the gospel has its own anarchic propensities.

Second, the Christian story offers an alternative vision to be served by such resistance and its anarchic directions: the rule of God as a reign of justice and peace. This is a radical alternative to the vision of the wider society. In its practices the church is to manifest an intrinsic relationship to the reign of God. Its practices are to be characterized by the covenantal commitment and justice that characterize God's rule.

I do not think here of some impossible ideal beyond any relative realization in actual life. Rather, I think of a story involving Ron Preuss in a church in Atlanta and the response of that church to the problem confronted by a member there. She was a working person in a job where she was constantly being harassed sexually by her employer. She was not well-to-do and could not afford to quit. She went to see Ron about the problem. After talking it through with him she called her boss to tell him she was quitting and why. She was able to do so because Ron promised that the church would help her find a new job and stand by her until she was employed again. That's exactly what they did. The capacities of the church to stand with working people in resistance to the principalities and powers are relatively unexplored in this kind of ministry. I believe they are enormous.

Third, in service to the rule of God the church becomes an alternative community, a material, substantive group of people whose embodied practices of faithfulness and resistance form and shape a new people. In this sense the church is a community of resistance itself and one of alternative formation. It is difficult to exaggerate how important it is for the church to be a different space, a place apart, a community of people who stand in sharp contrast to the wider world. As such it creates a sacred world different from and alternative to the status quo. This in itself can be a form of resistance of the first order where a different politics is in place. It is also a place where persons are formed by such practices and where we become a new people.

At this point the question of the nation-state looms large on the horizon of the working-class world. There can be no question that working people have their full share of patriotism. As with country music it sometimes takes on idolatrous proportions. At the same time, there is a deep distrust of government in both working people and country music, as I have suggested above.

In another work I have discussed patriotism as a deep sense of indebtedness by working people for all that the land and its people have meant to them.[3] I still believe this. I also believe that a deep love of place is an appropriate implication of the doctrine of creation in the Christian faith. It does not involve hatred of other places, but it certainly can mean a profound sense of one's rootage in a place and gratitude for it. This is the aspect of working-class love of country that the church can endorse and support.

At the same time I question any patriotism that endorses the nation as much more than an extrinsic commitment, that is, the nation is basically a tool, a means to other ends. It deserves nothing like the kind of commitment and worship so often extended to it in this society. Government can be supported when it works, when it is the best way to serve its people, but not when it uses its people for its own ends and for the ends of the few at the expense of the many. Let me be clear, too, that this is no backdoor move to support states rights in the U.S. context. I distrust the states even more than I do the federal government. States rights is often used as a pretext for an implicit racism and for an all-out assault on the poor, especially children, in this society.

There is a fundamental grasp of this issue by many working people who distrust government. A wedge needs to be driven between love of country and an uncritical allegiance to the nation-state. I believe that working people are open to such a sharp cleavage. A sensitivity is growing to the fact that our national government does not basically serve working people, but is increasingly given over to the interests of power and wealth. The church as an alternative community with an ultimate allegiance to Christ and not to the nation is an important antidote to the poisons of the nation-state that is bound to late capitalism.

Fourth, at the personal level the demeaning of working-class lives is one of the most devastating injuries of class. The church as alternative "trashy" community provides new definitions of what constitutes moral character, and what it is to be worthy and virtuous. The values and ideology of the world can be turned upside down. New definitions of what is valuable can be embodied in the practices of the church. The church becomes a community where alternative constructions of what it means to be a person, what it means to be virtuous, and what it means to be of good character are developed and championed. It can provide a substantive spirituality where people who are no people become God's people, where the "low and despised," the "trashy," are chosen.

The United States today is basically committed to a winner religion. If being "Number One" is not the major idol of the larger society, it is among the most to be adored in the American pantheon. In such a culture worth is tied to achievement. We earn our value on this basis. The Christian faith, however, proclaims that our worth comes from God as a gift. Further, life together is not a contractual relationship that allows us merely to seek our human rights in a mutual reciprocity. It is a covenantal reality in which faithfulness to one another and a commitment to an ultimate good frames our lives and defines our practices. The church claims that each and every person is made in the image of God. It proclaims a dignity and a value for people not reducible to their function and not dependent on the definitions of an achievement culture.[4]

Fifth, in keeping with the work of indigenous ministry the church will be coterminous with its parish. Here the church must bridge the chasm between the congregation and the wild side of life, between traditional morality and hard living. Part of this involves showing the desperation and loneliness of life on the edge of chaos and in the honky-tonk, but another part is to display the positive work of festivity and celebration there. It also means that the honky-tonk and other gathering places of working people are part of the regular visitation and presence of clergy and lay leadership, that is, it is a place where pastors and congregation are highly visible. Sensitive and empathic relationships with bar owners, waiters and waitresses, and country music performers as well as with customers are crucial. Authentic chaplaincy in these settings offers a radically different image of the church, one clearly needed.

In teaching the course on white soul, we have had a number of students who established chaplainlike relations with several honky-tonks in the Kansas City area. These students without exception express not only the importance but also the satisfactions of this kind of ministry.

Let it be clear, too, that no such trashy church will be free of complicity, compromise, and accommodation to the dominant culture.[5] These seem inescapable. The church that attempts to be in but not of the world will inevitably find itself, in part, captive to that world. But cultural captivity is not total, and resistance and populist anarchism become crucial practices to a church that opposes conformity to the world. We are at the beginning of such a work, but the everyday practices of working-class people have a long history and a lot of wisdom. Moreover, the church has within its story a wide range of practices to challenge the principalities and powers, and the redemptive work of the Spirit ever goes before us. The working-class church can by the power of God live its life in challenge to the dominant order and in the hope of a reign that will come.

These efforts require ways of doing theology that are different from the more literate expression I have given them in this section. The move will be from a literate style to one that is more oral. This is a distinctive style of doing theology, one not given adequate attention in the academy or the church. We can only begin such an approach here. I have given this more consideration in another work, but we can look at a few basic directions.[6]

Chapter 11
Doing Theology with Country Music

My Uncle J. L., hooked on pills and booze and caught in a nagging and unrelieved despair about the ice-pick damages to his dignity, sat in his living quarters at the small creosote plant he owned. During a long night he stuck the barrel of a .38-caliber pistol in his mouth, and pulled the trigger. The ammunition was so old the bullet never exited his skull, but, of course, it more than achieved its purpose.

After the funeral his sister, my Aunt Geneva, commented many times about a song by Kris Kristofferson. "You know," she said, "I wish so much I could have been there with him that night. If some of us had been there, we could've helped. I think of that song all the time: 'Help Me Make It Through the Night.' We could have helped him make it through that night."

Help Me Make It Through the Night

On first thought it is a strange use of that particular song. First recorded by Sammi Smith, the song begins with some very sexy lines. She invites a companion to a sexual liaison to last until dawn. She offers to let her hair play upon his skin the way the shadows play upon the wall. All of this is in order to "help me make it through the night."[1]

In verse 3 the singer indicates that she does not really care about "right or wrong," and she makes no attempt to under-stand the situation. As far as she's concerned the devil can have tomorrow because right now she is sad and alone and needs a friend. These lines are the ones that led one theologian to accuse this song of "defiant hedonism" and "self-conscious amoralism."[2]

But I think this is not a perceptive reading of the song. The last line of verse 3 and all of verse 4 can be understood as a prayer. The last line of the former begins with the word *Lord*, and states the need for a friend. Verse 4 then nails it: "Yesterday is dead and gone / And tomorrow's out of sight / And it's sad to be alone / Help me make it through the night."[3] What we have here is not defiant hedonism but abject despair, not amoralism but a bankrupt desperation. The past is dead and tomorrow is beyond view.

These are the things my Aunt Geneva heard in the song. She associated them with her brother. I can assure you that my aunt had no sexual images in mind when she heard this song in relation to him. The song spoke to her in another way and powerfully so. I had several conversations with her about it. Her response to it speaks volumes about a theology of country music and how working people use it in a profoundly spiritual way. She heard the desperation and the despair, not hedonism and amoralism. Out of her own life, which was not an easy one, she knew intimately the practices of making it through the night. She had made it through many nights of depression and hopelessness herself. To her the song spoke so clearly to the need for people you love to help you make it through. Her brother loved her; she loved him. She just knew that if she had been there he would have made it till morning came.

I have read this song several hundred times. I am struck by the fact that there is nothing in it anywhere that suggests that the yesterdays and tomorrows will be different after you make it through the night. I can find no guarantees in times past or times to come where there's a promise that things will be different. I pressed my Aunt Geneva on this. Her answer was straightforward but did not relieve my question. She said: "That's not the point. You just gotta make it through the night."

She never said it explicitly, but I began to understand something of what she meant. It is the one thing so astounding about the song. The crazy, unstated hope in a world where the past is dead and the future is irrelevant is the fact that the song never questions whether it is worth making it through the night. The song rests on an unexplicated trust that whether it is justified by the circumstances or not, getting through the hard night is worth it. It is a desperate form of choosing life.

A few years later Aunt Geneva died in her sleep in the early hours of the morning. She did not make it through that night. Yet, because of her sense of the importance of making it through, I find a strange and paradoxical hope in her passing. Her hearing of that song is an aching instance of choosing life and of going on.

It reminds me of what I heard so much in my life about "hunkerin' down," that is, a kind of basic endurance under the most difficult circumstances. It is a capacity to take it and still decide to live. Sometimes it is the claiming of a relationship, as in the song, when nothing else is there. Other times it takes the form of dealing with an opponent by "staring the sonofabitch in the face," determined finally not to give in but to hold out and hold on.

This aspect of country music and working-class life is sometimes characterized as stoic acquiescence; theologically it is seen as a form of last-ditch works righteousness. Surely this is external criticism. One needs to look more closely at the practice of hunkerin' down itself. Those I have known argue that times come when no other real option is available. It's the only thing you can do other than kill yourself. But it is more than this choice alone. Something in the practice of hunkerin' down itself is redemptive. I believe it is a residence of grace. Something happens in the practice that is not available otherwise. It cannot be known externally, which is the reason it is so often misread and miscategorized as some form of psychological escape or ego defense. On this point we have a lot to learn from country music and from working people. Clearly, hunkerin' down is not always a good response, but working people surely know this as well as others do.

Trust and Implicit Knowing

In this connection several points can be made about how country music is to be apprehended theologically. The first thing is to appreciate that country music will often assume or defend an unstated trust rather than attempt to articulate conceptual clarity and theoretical coherence. It is not systematic. To expect it to be so is to be disappointed. The music deals with coping and survival, with trust and hope, with faith and holding on. It does not do analysis but rather "shows," displays, and puts on view the coping, the survival, the trust, and the hope.

Second, the music works with implicit knowing. It is not a "literal reading"—whatever that is—too much is going on to be so simply accounted for. To hear it "literally" is to miss the use of the music made by working people. The very coin of its linguistic economy is story and proverb, not propositional accuracy and certainly not the correspondence of a statement with a theological position. "Help Me Make It Through the Night" has a proverbial quality to it. At the least the words seemed to be deeply embedded in the practices of my Aunt Geneva. It was a saying that was employed in the practices of her life but articulated no systematic point of view as such. At the same time, those who get their ideas consistent and coherent would do well to appreciate the enormity of her capacity to cope and survive and to live with trust and hope even to the end.

Third, there are plenty of places for critique of country music theologically. Sometimes the songs seem to place God and the faith at the periphery of life, meaning in part that God is called upon only when trouble comes. Sometimes the faith is so personalized that it has no sense of a community of faith and its resources, in part a testimony to the failing of the church but surely not reducible to this alone. One must never forget the commercial intentions of the producers of country music. These will not be wiped away from the lyrics and the music and will not likely ever fully square with a wider range of the demands of faith and the church's responsibility to issues of witness, justice, and peace. The music sometimes voices, as we see above, a covert, if not overt racism, sexism, and even classism. For example, even Dolly Parton can sometimes write and sing an awfully bad line, to wit: "That one is only poor, only if they choose to be."[4] It is a grotesquely insensitive thing to say and not in keeping with virtually the entire range of everything else she does.

The use of country music theologically depends a great deal on selection. There is so much rich material in the music that one does not have to use the stuff that is really theologically bad, except to make the point of how tacky it is.

Finally, there is a great deal of explicitly religious music in country: like "The Great Speckled Bird," "I'll Fly Away," "Will the Circle Be Unbroken," and many, many more. A few of these are great songs, but I have not focused here on these religious songs for two reasons. I believe the best music theologically is not in the "sacred songs" of the genre, but in those that deal with the concrete lives of working people. For example, I find much more theological value in Kristofferson's "Sunday Morning Coming Down" than I do in Red Foley's "Peace in the Valley." Second, I am writing here to reach people the church usually does not. In my experience such folk do not find the religious music as related to their lives, as gritty, and as explicit about work, love, standing up to the SOBs, living with unresolved contradictions, and making it through the night. I believe that one of the reasons Hank Williams could not get Saturday night and Sunday morning together was because he did not see the spiritual—and I would say theological—significance of Saturday night. Moreover, a basic part of the problem is the failure of the church to deal with this same issue.

In saying these things I do not want to dismiss those churches that have combined gospel music and country in myriad ways. Too many working people have made it through the night with a faith built and sustained there. At the same time these churches are too often communities of true believers who embody a respectability and the controls attendant to it that repel the mass of working people in deep resistance to the official world. Churches that deal with the principalities and powers by establishing islands of respectability in congregations of true believers do not reach the depths of an angular populist insurgency and pave over the deep fissures of a world that won't come out right.

To Look the Turtle in the Eye

Basic to theology is the questioning of the adequacies of human trusts. The ability to sniff out an idol, to trace the fault lines of a misplaced confidence, and to disclose the backsides of pretentious "saviors" certainly are among the first of the critical works of prophetic religious thought. Indeed, if our lives do rest on trust and we finally come to the place where it is turtles all the way down, then theology has a responsibility to raise sharp questions with these basic trusts. Country music offers ways to look the turtle in the eye and to question its reliability.

Religion is a sensitive issue in the music, and criticism of it is usually dealt with carefully. As a result country will typically approach the subject with humor. Curtis Ellison points out that a basic theme of country humor is to gain some respite from "the emphasis on personal salvation associated with evangelical religion."[5] Taking on an overwrought piety is a frequent theme.

A deflation of piety is delightfully displayed in Ray Stevens's "Mississippi Squirrel Revival," where some kids accidentally let loose one of those furry creatures during morning worship at "The First Self-Righteous Church of Pascagoula." As the squirrel scampers through the congregation, scrambling up pant legs and dresses, the members believe that some radical visitation of the Spirit has come upon them and begin to confess sin even to the point of naming names! Such humor would doubtlessly relieve some congregations anticipating another long homily, but such a song can be the occasion for entry into a more serious discussion of sanctimonious pretensions.[6]

Jerry Clower tells one of his wonderful stories, "The Dead Cat," in which a bereaved woman takes her deceased pet complete with a casket to two different churches asking for a Christian burial. Having been refused at both places she goes to a Baptist church. When the preacher there protests her even thinking that his church would bury a cat, she says "Well, I'm frustrated, and I am prepared to give two thousand dollars to whoever holds a service for my cat." With that the preacher exclaims, "Lady, why didn't you tell me your cat was a Baptist?"[7] One should not miss in such stories the possibilities for critique of the church's own lust for the lucrative. A story like Clower's opens the door for sharp questioning but uses humor to lessen the defensiveness that can often attend such critique. .

Will There Be Mogen David in Heaven?

Sometimes a song has an ache even in the midst of very funny lines. But the mixture of pain and humor has a long history as a site for rich theological work. Larry Gatlin and the Gatlin Brothers sing a song called "The Midnight Choir." Not only does it depict the plight of the homeless, but it also reports an eye-opening Eucharist that poses a question sharply awaiting an ultimate answer.

> The doors to the mission open at seven
> And the soup will be ready about nine
> Right now it's six-thirty
> They're ragged and dirty
> They're standin' and sittin' and layin' in line
> First they'll do a little singin'
> Then hear a little preachin'
> And get saved for the third time this week
> A bowl of soup later and a pat on the shoulder
> And by midnight they're back on the street.

From the mission they find an alley and "an old buddy with a bottle of heaven" that "means everything / One bottle for four, Thank God someone scored / And now the midnight choir starts to sing":

> Will they have Mogen David in heaven . . . oh yeah
> Dear Lord, we'd all like to know
> Will they have Mogen David in heaven . . . sweet Jesus
> If they don't, who the hell wants to go?[8]

I hope the moralisms of Christians are not aroused by such surface profanation, one that covers a deeply sacred struggle that touches everyone. It is, moreover, a paraphrase of a deeply biblical question: Is there a balm in Gilead? Is there healing? One must remember here, too, that country music, like theology, is not univocal, and more than one thing can be heard. Remember, the enemy at the Last Supper was not those suffering some genetic thirst, it was not the poor searching for balm, it was not the few sitting in confusion before Christ and the mysterious events that would befall him and them in the next three days. Yes, for the midnight choir, Mogen David means the quieting of jangled nerves yearning for a fix, but it also takes on ultimacy for the healing of the nations. To see into the tacitly understood faith of people who do not engage in the whipsaws of academic hermeneutics but rather who cope and survive and, strangely, hope in God is to witness a trust, or at least the yearning for a trust, that is finally the only foundation any of us truly has. If there is finally no answer, no healing, then, indeed, who the hell wants to go?

Crucifixion and Resurrection

It is important to see in country music a struggle, often covered with humor, to address this issue of basic trust. Where the world is so often unresponsive to your efforts, but demeans you and your life in basic everyday encounters, then this issue of trust cannot be approached apart from the activity of life itself. Trust is not merely a psychological characteristic; it is the grounding base of one's life and practice. It is not so much articulated as done. It is not so much the conscious makeup of one's subjectivity as the very cast of one's bearing. It is what gets you up in the morning, what keeps you on the job, what enables you to hunker down, what keeps you finally in love with your family or leads you to leave it, it is what gets you through the night. It is a trust formed in some story of how the world is, sometimes a very latent and implicit narrative. Sometimes with working people it is a story of desperation and despair about a world where the best you can do is get by. Sometimes it is a story of going through the motions and living numb. Any attempt to address the faith that does not come to terms with this struggle and the often unarticulated trust activated in it will not engage the lived lives of working people. Such efforts will be abstract, irrelevant, and, worst of all, not seriously attempt to discern the redemptive work of the Spirit in their everyday activity. My deepest confidence in country music as the embodiment of working-class life, with all of its limitations, is that it, indeed, addresses this dimension of the working world.

In the midst of this kind of struggle country music sings a theology of *failure*. It comes from and speaks to people who are "born to lose." Some say it is soap opera put to music because it tells stories, stories that confront life so concretely and so painfully that its renditions of the ragged edges of time sing the songs and the feelings of people in heartbreak hotels, honky-tonks, walled prisons, dead-end marriages, hopeless jobs, lost homes of long ago, and empty Sundays coming down. The music's terrain is one of good men and bad and of cowboys who "ain't easy to love and are harder to hold." It is a place of strong, fine women and of "good girls" who are "gonna go bad" and "take their love to town." It lives on the edge of and in the hell of the wild side of life. It knows hard living ain't hardly livin' at all.[9]

But it is more than the display of sin and loss because it is a *theology* of failure. Smack-dab crowded with faith it almost always "says more than it says," and no matter how hard the day or how long the night, some hint of hope or some clue of a protest claims, if not a certain future, a signal of something *more*—that somehow, someday, somewhere will keep the circle from being broken. In blind desperation folks still see the light. These are among the reasons it is such a fine resource for theology because one finds there the full range of despair and hope, of life and death, of the marks of our mortality and the strange longing that will not let us go.

Finally, of course, it offers an important resource in the life and work of the church with working people. When the rituals of deference and demeanor of the wider society become the radical sharing of bread and wine in the Eucharist, a new reality is born and a new definition of what it means "to be somebody" comes into existence. When the church is known as the community that opposes the distortions of "official truth," the door is opened to hear the Word of Jesus Christ. When a life of taking orders is countered by a congregation of hospitality and mutual respect, when a community of faith becomes a free zone, an open space in a culture of captivity, when the valuations of the world are turned upside down, when the self-elevations of supremacist tastes, language, etiquette, affect, and lifestyles are countered by an honoring of indigenous practices, when the church itself is a community of resistance against the external impositions and lifestyle colonialism of a dominant order, and when the idols of Caesar are met with an anarchism committed to Christ, then the church is an alternative people of embodied practices intrinsic to the Reign of God.

Wind and Fire at the Starlite Club

When Larry Hollon and I teach the white soul course, we require the students to spend several nights in honky-tonks where working people gather. For many years my favorite place was the Starlite Club, now closed. Located on the back end of a gravel lot the size of a football field it was a popular gathering place, always full when the weekdays got closer to the weekend.

It was the last night of the course before the last class the next day. We always tried to do something together on the last night. So Larry and I suggested the Starlite Club and described it as a very down-home place. When the class ended, three African American students came over to me. They looked hesitantly at one another, seeming to want one of the others to speak first. Finally, John did:

"Tex, we're enjoying the course and we know the trips at night are important, and we want to cooperate with the class process, but . . . we're . . . not . . . sure we ought to go to the Starlite Club. We might not be welcome there."

"I see what you mean," I answered, trying to think fast for a good answer because I really wanted them to go, and in all the years we have been going out we only had one problem, and that with a waitress who seemed to ignore the table with the black students.

"Well, I can't guarantee you that there won't be a problem." I felt so mealymouthed with that comment that I said the next thing that popped into my mind:

"But if you go, and there's trouble, I'll take the first punch." (Have you ever done something and, as soon as you did it, you wished you could take it back? I am not a brave man, and I had not taken a punch in years. I'd probably disintegrate! But I had said it.)

Basically they looked at their feet and then up at one another with very quick glances at me in between. I knew what they were thinking, at least I thought I did. I imagined them saying to themselves: "Look, this guy is middle-aged, he's going to take a punch. And remember, he's from Mississippi. Do you really think he would take a punch for us?" I could tell they were anxious, but by then I had difficulty believing they were more apprehensive than I. Finally one of the three looking for agreement from the others broke the silence:

"You'll take the first punch?"

Well it was too late to back out then, and I nodded in agreement trying to look a lot more confident than I was. We made plans for an arrival time, and I agreed to be there early.

Believe you me, I was! I reserved a table and got a couple of other students to sit with me to keep it. As soon as the three African American men came through the door, I was on my feet, shaking their hands and welcoming them to the table.

We sat down, the waitress came by and everything seemed fine. I was feeling better. The band was especially good that night, and I never heard them when they were bad. It was a down-home country band. So much so that the lead guitar fretted with his left hand upside down.

The band had been playing country rock and then began to play a nice slow dance, known as a "belly rubber." In the class that year was a woman with very blonde hair, really a kind of bright yellow, which made her visible from anywhere in that relatively dark room. I had suspected that she was no great fan of mine, and my suspicions were fulfilled when she came over and asked one of the black guys to dance! They did.

I can remember my heart pounding as I said to myself with no little resignation: "I'm gonna get hit."

There was a little stir at one table, mainly a comment or two that hardly anyone else noticed. They danced the longest two and a half minutes of my life, the song ended, they sat down, and nothing happened.

I was feeling better. As I recall I was even sitting higher in my chair, my courage seeming to be much stronger since it did not appear that I would have to demonstrate it.

Then the band started to play "Georgia." The spouse of Bob, one of the three African Americans, was named Georgia. She was back at the parish, and he was missing her. So he borrowed a sweater from that same blonde woman, draped one sleeve over his arm, took the other sleeve in his hand and danced through the number all by himself. It was clear that I was in cardiac arrest, as I said to myself: "Now I know I'm gonna get hit!"

But nothing happened. No one seemed to notice or care. My apprehension seemed utterly groundless. The longer I sat there, the more ashamed I was that I had projected all that bigotry and violence into the working men and women at the Starlite Club. I don't mean to suggest there was no racism there. It pervades our society. Still, it did not take the form I was so fearful it would.

Some ten minutes later the band started to play "Under the Double Eagle." It was magnificent. If you can sit still when a good country band plays that tune, do not go to the physician, you are dead already.

That year we also had a Native American in the class, who at that point got up, went out on the floor and began to do the dangdest combination of tribal and kicker dances I ever saw. With that everybody in that room got up and circled the floor to watch Rich, the Native American, and an Anglo woman do their stuff. They were not dancing together, but rather, each one was doing a distinctively different style.

She was about five feet tall and weighed about two hundred pounds, and could she dance! Her dress was silver and outlined in a kind of silver brocade that was even brighter than the fabric. In each ear she had an earring with a light in it. Every time she bounced, the lights blinked because they were attached to a battery . . . somewhere! Meanwhile, they had a strobe light on the bandstand and every time it flashed, her silver dress exploded in light. She looked like a duel between fireflies and lightning: blink, blink . . . zwoosha . . . blink, blink . . . zwoosha . . . blink, blink . . . zwoosha!

By now everyone gathered together in one place around the dance floor and clapped to the beat of "Under the Double Eagle." I couldn't help engaging in a bit of hyperbole, saying to myself: "Everybody in the known world is here." It was then that I knew what the sound of a mighty wind from heaven was at Pentecost: it was "Under the Double Eagle." As I looked around the room, I could see tongues of fire distributed on everyone . . . silver tongues of fire. Each person was shouting in his and her native idiom and yet everyone was hearing the other in the language of celebration.

Someone will say: "Aw, they were full of booze." I think not. The Starlite Club could have been a place of rejection and violence. If anything, booze is more conducive to violence than acceptance. The Starlite Club could have been closed; instead it was open. It surely was not the reign of God, it was doubtless not without ambiguity, but people came together in festivity who often do not. On that night hostility did not win, hospitality did.

This moment from nearly twenty years ago moves me and haunts me. It moves me as a foretaste of what I believe is the destiny of the world, but it haunts me because it seems so distant from the walls of hostility that divide us, the divisions of race and gender and class. The principalities and powers still seem to rule the day. But as long as we can dream and imagine a different world, as long as we can resist and find in broken celebrations time to live the truth and be different, as long as people can sing from their hearts and ache to make it through the night, as long as the Spirit wedges its ways into festive hospitality, silver dresses, tribal dances, and soul music, the future is not done.

Appendix

A'Pickin' and A'Sangin':
A Short History of
Country Music

Bill Malone observes that both country musicians and their "core audience" have been "working people—farmers, mill operatives, mechanics, coal miners, oil workers, truck drivers, sales clerks, cooks, waitresses, beauticians—whose roots and value systems lie, preponderantly, in the fundamentalist rural South."[1] Yet, he goes on to say that "Country music has moved well beyond its original regional parameter as it has become a major voice of lower- and middle-class people throughout America."[2] This story is the focus of this appendix.

1922-1932
The Birth of an Industry: Hillbilly Beginnings

The music began in the white rural South. Originally called "old-fashioned music" or "songs from Dixie" or "old familiar tunes" it was Ralph Peer who first used the term "hillbillies" in 1925 in reference to a group of mountain musicians he recorded. The term was picked up and applied to the music as a genre.[3] In the thirties, with the coming of the singing cowboys and the work of Bob Wills, the name "Western" would be added. The term "country music" did not come along until the late 1940s.[4] After that it was known as country music or as country western.

In 1922 Eck Robertson did the first documented commercial hillbilly record. This commercial form came into being, in part, as a result of a communication revolution that brought radio and phonograph records into general use in that decade. With the development of the 78-rpm record, A & R (artists and repertoire) men like Ralph Peer, Frank Walker, Eli Oberstein, Art Satherley, and Jack Kapp, along with their recording crews, spread across the cities of the South looking for talent. They found a diverse group. Some, like Fiddlin' John Carson and Riley Puckett, had something of a reputation for having worked on radio in the region. A few others, like Uncle Dave Macon, had performed on the vaudeville stage. Mostly, however, they had performed at community functions: everything from fish fries to house parties, from hawking ballads at events as varied as county fairs and fiddling contests, from reunions of various kinds to working tent and medicine shows.[5]

From its beginnings country music has been dominated by men with fateful results for women. Consistent with this fact, Mary Bufwack and Robert Oermann contend that "the story of country music is a window into the world of the majority of American women." It is a story of struggle, of "poverty, hardship, economic exploitation, sexual subjugation, and limited opportunities." But it is also a story of resistance to these very adversities and captivities. Songs of exaltation, of protest, of "joyful rebellion" also characterize women's participation in the music. In the early days a woman could be in a traveling act only as a member of a performer family.[6]

With this array of men and women performers and events it is evident that country music did not drop out of the sky or suddenly come into existence in the twenties. Its roots go way back and it is indebted to a wide variety of sources. James R. Morris calls country music "an amalgam of influences." For example, the structure of the music—a verse followed by a thirty-two-bar chorus of AABA form—came from Europe. Its harmonic structure and melodic pattern were derived from the popular song, the show tune, and the church hymn with elaborations on this melodic sequence coming from blues and gospel. Its rhythms originated in English country dances, the polka, the schottische, the Ländler waltzes of Germany and Austria, the barn dance and the jig. Its direct, even blunt and sometimes crude engagement with life and its joy and hardship, along with ingredients of "satire, cynicism, and wish fulfillment," are evidence of African American influences. The range of instrumentation came out of Britain, Western Europe, and Africa. In its use of the guitar, the fiddle, banjo, mandolin, bass, dobro, pedal steel guitar, and harmonica and in the ways they are played—"struck with flat picks, twanged with finger picks, scraped with the bow, or flailed with the fingers"—Morris notes a further indebtedness to African American influence. In that performers often compose their own music and develop close, almost personal, relationships with their audiences, country music is reminiscent of the minstrel tradition of the Middle Ages. Morris sums up country music as "a synthesis of materials" common to the culture. It is deeply indebted to black culture for its "sound, structure and text." In composition the spirituals and the blues are basic materials in its construction, and its harmonic origins can be found in the blues. Its rhythms came from white culture, echoing English and European country dances in their earlier forms. Its text grew in part from "the fervor of the southern Protestant pulpit" but also from the vernacular of "the bar rooms and roadside cafes," and from the storytelling and events of the oral culture from which it came.[7]

Its emergence in the twenties among white rural working people came at a hard time. The economy deteriorated, with cotton dropping from 43 cents to 11 cents a pound. By the end of the decade half of the farmers did not own the land they worked, and in 1932 twenty thousand farms were foreclosed a month.[8] Still, the music prospered and did so with a move from the phonograph to the radio. In 1922, record sales hit 100 million units. During the late twenties and early thirties (1927 to 1932), however, they dropped from sales of 104 million to 6 million units annually. Meanwhile, in 1929 one-third of the homes in the nation owned radios.[9] Radios were cheaper, had a better sound, and played continuously.

The twenties and early thirties brought the Carter Family and their "values of home and family, decency and modesty"[10] expressed in a style that suggested a small intimate circle of family and friends. It was a style and format that identified itself with a traditional morality and religious faith that would influence many country artists to follow.

Yet, this was also the era of Jimmie Rodgers. A former brakeman for the railroad, hailing from just outside Meridian, Mississippi, he could praise traditional values, but he embodied the fascination of the open road and the life of the ramblin' man. Dying in 1933 at thirty-six years of age of tuberculosis, "the poet's disease,"[11] he became a mythic figure virtually in his own time and established a style that many country artists would emulate in the years to follow.[12] The ramblin' man theme would echo in the music in the decades to follow in styles like honky-tonk music, the Outlaw Movement, the New Traditionalists, and others.

This juxtaposition of tradition and a ramblin' lifestyle grew, at least in part, from the geographical and social dislocation of the times. The twentieth century can be seen as a century of dislocation. For example, there were nearly 32 million farms with 30.1 percent of the population in 1920; by 1970 there were 9.7 million farms with 4.8 percent of the population.[13] The farm population continued to drop and counted less than 4.6 million in 1990.[14] The change from a rural to an industrial to an info-technological society had fateful consequences for working people. The move from rural America to the cities and, for some, to the suburbs was a story of dislocation and separation. Country music must be understood against the backdrop of this transition. No genre of music in the United States had given expression to this transition for white working Americans as profoundly as country music.

1933-1940
Survival of a Music: Depression and Dissemination
Many working people entered depression long before the stock market collapsed in 1929, but the Great Depression brought even harder times. Wages and the ranks of the employed steadily declined from 1929 to 1933. Twenty-eight percent of the households in the country did not have even a single employed worker, and three-fourths of the households only had a part-time wage earner. Urban dwellers ransacked garbage dumps for food. Rural people lived on dandelions and blackberries and other make-do sources for food. Working people climbed on railroad cars and traveled around the country looking for work. Hunger, homelessness, and destitution stalked the land, and a deepening anger and agitation took political forms in union organizing, strikes, and in socialist and communist movements. Singers like Aunt Molly Jackson,

Sarah Ogun Gunning, and Florence Reece sang to the social ills and evils of capitalism and the depression.

Between 1935 and 1939, 350,000 Dust Bowl farmers went to California looking for relief from Depression woes and farm failure. In 1936, 175,000 of them lived in shanties and tents in camps for working people set up by the government. In California they met exploitation, oppression, disease, bigotry, and backbreaking labor. Country music was one way the workers dealt with this hard desperation. Rose Maddox came out of this migration and becomes a key figure in the development of honky-tonk and rockabilly music. This geographical movement also established California as a center for the music, especially Bakersfield.[15]

While the careers of some of the pioneers of country music recording ended with the depression, the music survived and reached out to an even larger audience. The coming of radio served a new era of country music. Not only was there the development of large radio stations in the United States but also even larger ones along the border of Mexico, which were not subject to the watt power limits of U.S. regulation. By 1938 radio was in 82 percent of U.S. homes.[16]

With the radio the National Barn Dances sprung up around the country. During the thirties the largest and most important of these was the one at WSL in Chicago, which began in 1924 and reached significant audiences in the 1930s. The singing cowboys of the silver screen came along in this period: Gene Autry, Tex Ritter, Roy Rogers, Rex Allen, and Bob Nolan and the Sons of the Pioneers. In 1935, Patsy Montana recorded "I Want to Be a Cowboy's Sweetheart," which became the first record by a country music woman artist to sell a million copies. New songwriters and artists appeared, and the music took on a Southwest coloration with the coming of Bob Wills and his Light Crust Doughboys, later the Texas Playboys. Bill Malone points out that during these times the use of cowboy and mountaineer images in country music helped to counteract the more negative images of rural and urban working people.[17]

Discoveries of oil in Texas and in Oklahoma and the repeal of Prohibition in 1933 helped generate a dancing and listening public. These innovations in turn brought new instrumentation like electric and acoustic guitars, pianos, drums, and horns. Western music continued on throughout this century, and "country western" endured as a basic name for the increasingly new sounds of the music.[18]

1941-1953
The Honky-Tonk Era: Country Music Enters the Cities
World War II brought a dispersal of working people across the country and around the world. Many were in military service, and others went to jobs in defense industries. The result of these large migrations was dislocation, the weakening of family ties, lessening of traditional constraints on women and children, and a changing socioeconomic sta-

tus. Country music went with these migrations and began to reflect the wider world working people experience. Ted Daffan's "Born to Lose" cried out all over the country and even in distant parts of the world where G.I.s were stationed.

The struggle of country music's "traditional soul" with "new and modern realities" reflected the loneliness, dislocation, and separation of the war.[19] The jukebox came into its own in the mid-thirties and many soldiers found solace in songs that sang his and, in a changing world, her life. Roy Acuff, from the mountains of East Tennessee, achieved prominent stardom in these years, so much so that in a banzai charge on Okinawa the Japanese soldiers shouted what they thought would be the worst of insults: "To hell with Roosevelt; to hell with Babe Ruth; to hell with Roy Acuff!"[20]

Still, the sounds of the Southwest dominated the jukeboxes with the offerings of Jimmie Davis, Al Dexter, Ted Daffan, Gene Autry, Cliff Brunner, Bob Wills, and Ernest Tubb. When Tubb joined the Grand Ole Opry in 1943, his association presaged the integration of the southeastern and southwestern styles that would characterize the immediate postwar years.

During the war, women entered the work force in large numbers, and female artists in country music benefited from greater opportunities to entertain as morale-boosting performers and gained from this greater independence and confidence. Women DJs, performers, composers, promoters, and others emerged during these years. Artists like Minnie Pearl and composers like Cindy Walker, perhaps the greatest at her talent in the history of the music, emerged in the war years.[21]

Following the war, country music found great commercial success. New record companies, radio stations, and live shows started around the country. The Grand Ole Opry that had begun in 1925 came into pre-eminence as a radio barn dance show, followed by others like the Louisiana Hayride in Shreveport. The Grand Ole Opry and the city of Nashville would become increasingly the center of country music.

The postwar years were a time of increasing prosperity for many working-class people. Yankelovich reports that the median family income of U.S. Americans more than doubled in the twenty-to twenty-five-year period following World War II. Judith Stacey notes that this was the brief period in which working-class people were able to develop what she calls the modern family: a breadwinner father, a homemaker mother who stayed home, and their dependent minor child. This would come to an end beginning in the mid-sixties with the loss of high paying working-class jobs with good benefits.[22]

The most important development during this period was honky-tonk music, though getting this name only in the 1960s. "No phenomenon has been more influential in divesting country music of its pastoral identification, or of suggesting its increasing working-class affiliation."[23] Honky-tonk music brought new instrumentation and a new array of artists like Floyd Tillman, Hank Thompson, Webb Pierce, and Lefty Frizzell. The music deals not only with the honky-tonk, but also with the wider world of the working class, with city life, with the relations of love, family, and work—and with these the increasing problems of cheating, alcohol, and divorce. Great stylists appeared in these years. Joining Thompson, Tillman, and Frizzell were artists like Hank Snow, Slim Whitman, Kitty Wells, Molly O'Day, and Rose Maddox.[24]

The greatest singer of this era and perhaps of all time was Hank Williams from Alabama. With a profoundly expressive voice, he ranged across the spectrum of styles: country boogie, blues, yodeling, and gospel. He had an enormous capacity for emotional realism that could say in song what his listeners feel. His short meteoric career and tragic life without success in love and dogged by chronic and compulsive drinking made him a legend following his death in 1953.[25] After his life many male country singers would follow his style and develop variations on it. He was a key figure in the development of the tradition.

1953-1960
The Cost of Success: Rockabilly and Country Pop

In 1950 Patti Page demonstrated the crossover commercial potential of country music when done in a pop style with her rendition of "Tennessee Waltz." A number of Hank Williams's songs were turned into hits by popular singers like Tony Bennett, Frankie Laine, and Mitch Miller. But when Elvis Presley walked into Sun Records in 1954 and recorded "That's All Right, Mama" and "Blue Moon of Kentucky" he almost killed country music. Rock 'n' roll took over the country. Reeling from this blow from Elvis and others, country music artists began to adopt aspects of the rock 'n' roll style in a form that would be called rockabilly.

Meanwhile Chet Atkins, that masterful guitarist and RCA Records A & R executive, came up with a style of country music designed to appeal to a broader cross section of people. Variously called country pop, or "countrypolitan" or "the Nashville Sound," it created a music that is "essentially country in thematic content, and often in vocal sound, but was pop in instrumentation."[26]

Under the threat of extinction by rock 'n' roll, country pop seemed to take over the entirety of country music. While there were exceptions that continued more traditional sounds, country seemed permeated with smooth instrumentation, background singers, and an overabundance of "do ahs." This was not a distinguished time for country and not a time when the music reflected working-class life, at least in these Nashville Sound forms. Yet, of the artists of the period, Jim Reeves was perhaps the finest of the men.

But one female artist, Patsy Cline, seemed to rise above the limits of the Nashville Sound to take a permanent place among country's best. Her stardom, too, was brief, with a life marred by marital troubles, a near-lethal car wreck, and finally a tragic death in a plane crash in 1963 as she moved to the top of the country music world with no little success on the pop charts. Today, her standing in country music is far greater than when she was alive.[27]

Perhaps one of the lasting contributions of the Nashville Sound was the coming together of a group of women artists during this period through the important influence of Patsy Cline. It turned out to be a significant instance of the empowerment of women in the industry and in the music.

The Persistence of Tradition: Bluegrass and the Urban Folk Revival

Still, country music barely survived the coming of rock 'n' roll and its own turn to the Nashville Sound. The reinvigoration of country, in part, came from an external and unexpected source, the urban folk revival. This folk music movement triggered by songs like the Kingston Trio's "Tom Dooley" brought renewed interest to traditional songs. While the music was not strictly speaking "folk music," nevertheless it captured attention and a market for "authentic music."

This also brought an interest in bluegrass, the name applied to a kind of acoustic band that more or less followed the style pioneered in the 1940s by Bill Monroe. Originally bluegrass appealed to country music fans who resented the flood of rock 'n' roll and the new countrypolitan music. It became virtually a "homeless shelter" for traditional musicians of both a religious and a secular bent. When folk music was "discovered" by college students, however, bluegrass suddenly became popular and since has gone on to develop a range of forms from progressive to traditional. Still, however, it flourished outside the country mainstream and appeared primarily on small recording labels and at festivals. It was, says Bill Malone, "a quasi-religious commitment to, and preservation of, both a form of music and a way of life."[28]

1960-1972
The Reinvigoration of Modern Country Music

The coming of the sixties brought a reinvigoration of the music. Country music radio stations increased in numbers all over the country. The music gained a significant airing on television with shows starring Porter Wagoner, Jimmy Dean, Roger Miller, Glen Campbell, and Johnny Cash. *Hee Haw* had success as a "grotesque parody" of hillbilly life. Particularly important in the spread of country music was the Armed Forces Network,[29] and military personnel continued to prefer the music with 65 to 72 percent of base PX's record sales going to country.[30] More than that, the military and its personnel played a crucial role in the international distribution of the music, as indicated above.

These events occurred along with an emergent interest in traditional songs and styles: a renewed life for honky-tonk music, the emergence of the country historical or saga song, the previously mentioned folk music movement, and the surging influence of bluegrass. In this return to tradition artists like George Jones, Ray Price, Buck Owens, Merle Haggard led the way. Duets like Porter Wagoner and Dolly Parton, and Conway Twitty and Loretta Lynn also signaled a return to older styles, as did the music of Bill Anderson. Moreover, songwriters like Harlan Howard and songwriters and performers like Willie Nelson, Tom T. Hall, and Kris Kristofferson began to emerge as key people in the field. As the sixties drew to a close, Malone reports that the music had become "more self-consciously working class in image and orientation."[31]

The late fifties and sixties brought the Civil Rights movement and, following close behind, the Vietnam War and the coming of the counterculture. During these years country was no longer dominated by adult male white Protestants. Charley Pride was the first African American to be a country music superstar. While Deford Bailey performed in the early years of the Grand Ole Opry, he never achieved the level of Pride's fame. Freddy Fender and Johnny Rodriguez were stars who came out of the Hispanic community.[32] Moreover, while the traditional male-female pattern was endorsed in the music and the myth of domesticity was still preserved, a gradual women's revolution had begun. The pioneering work of people like Kitty Wells and the breakthroughs of Patsy Cline opened doors for artists like Loretta Lynn, Tammy Wynette, Dolly Parton, and for youthful initiatives by artists like Crystal Gayle.[33]

These breakthroughs, however, did not so much represent a shift in ideology as the industry's own commercial sense that it needed to broaden and to try new and bolder experimentation. Throughout the Vietnam War and the civil rights struggle one could still find Hank Snow supporting George Wallace, and Merle Haggard blasting the protestors in "Okie from Muskogee." By the end of the sixties, however, the music had become more expressive of working-class life with songs like Haggard's "Working Man's Blues" and Johnny Russell's "Rednecks, White Socks, and Blue Ribbon Beer."[34]

1972-1984
Commercial Success and the Struggle Between Tradition and Country Pop

The seventies brought new changes. The Grand Ole Opry moved from sacred old Ryman Auditorium in 1973, where it had been since 1941, to Opryland. The Association of Country Entertainers formed in 1974 to protest the naming of Olivia Newton-John as Female Singer of the Year by the Country Music Association. While short-lived, it reflected some of the struggle of country music with identity in these years of success. The ACE, however, was no purist band of traditionalists, not with country pop artists like Barbara Mandrell. Remaining strong, country pop was led by artists like Anne Murray, Don Williams, John Denver, Kenny Rogers, and Olivia Newton-John. Quartets like the Statler Brothers, the Oak Ridge Boys, and Alabama prospered, and a youth and young adult movement countered the Nashville Sound and preserved and revitalized traditional forms of the music. Meanwhile, some artists were moving from country to rock.[35]

In 1972 Willie Nelson left Nashville for Austin, Texas, and he and Waylon Jennings began the outlaw group, including other artists like Jerry Jeff Walker, Jessi Colter and Tompall Glaser. While the Outlaw Movement was largely a promotional move, drawing on a plurality of musical sources and reaching out to new publics, it nevertheless did "more to preserve a distinct identity for country music than most of their contemporaries who wear the 'country' label."[36] There was also a rebirth of cowboy music with songs like Marty Robbins's "El Paso" and Ed Bruce's "Mammas Don't Let Your Babies Grow Up to Be Cowboys." About the same time a new generation of honky-tonk singers appeared with artists like George Strait, Mel Street, Moe Bandy, Gene Watson, and John Anderson.

These years see the rise of Loretta Lynn's star as a female artist who made her name, in part, by standing up to men while Tammy Wynette was standing by hers. Getting her first hits in 1963, her songs on working-class experience as a coal miner's daughter and the struggles of working-class women are and will be classic in the country music tradition.[37]

At the same time the early seventies began a downward trend for working people. Wages started a steady decline in constant dollars that continued into the mid-nineties. This seems to have no effect on the commercial prospering of country music, however.

1985-1995
Contemporary Country Versus Neotraditionalism

From 1985 to 1993 record sales went from almost $440 million to $1.75 billion, and country music moved from a 10 percent share of the recorded-music market to a 17.5 percent share in these same years. If rock is still the most popular music in the U.S., country is the fastest growing. There are now 2,500 radio stations with a full-time country format. The music reaches 62 million homes on cable TV, and the music is almost constantly on view.[38] In 1990 *American Demographics* reports that 60 percent of all Americans listen to country artists.

With this has come a shift from the mostly rural and urban working people of previous years to a wider audience. As we see in the Introduction, 44 percent of the music's listeners are boomers, and 40 percent of the fans come from the three most upscale groupings in 1990.[39]

Into this opulence came the struggles between the New Traditionalists and Contemporary Country. Calling the latter the music's "most thorough self-evisceration yet," Tony Scherman describes its growing success in the early 1980s when, as he says, country "descended" with "the awful Kenny Rogers years, to an almost insufferable blandness, the emblem of its pasteurization Dolly Parton, with her eager passage from fresh-voiced singer-songwriter to Top 40 hack." Meanwhile, the neotraditionalists count as theirs Ricky Skaggs and Dwight Yoakam— "the most talented country singer to emerge in the eighties"—and Emmylou Harris, a convert to country who resists "sweetening her music."[40]

The first half of the nineties brought "the hunk" phenomenon with artists like Garth Brooks, Clint Black, and Billy Ray Cyrus, among others. Complaints surfaced from female artists that the relative neglect of women performers suggested too much of the patriarchy of earlier times. Reba McEntire continues to maintain a highly visible stardom, and relatively new stars like Kathy Mattea, Mary Chapin Carpenter, Lorrie Morgan, and Trisha Yearwood do as well. Meanwhile, Willie Nelson, Waylon Jennings, Merle Haggard, Kris Kristofferson, and Tom T. Hall, some of the greatest performers and songwriters in country music history, report difficulty in getting out recordings and making personal appearances in an industry so committed to young artists.

Some worry that, as successful as it was, country music as such is coming to an end. It has lost its original social location in the South and Southwest among rural people and is losing its relation to the urban working class. Its commercialization and pursuit of the affluent crossover market, especially with boomers and the young adult Generation X, means a serious confusion in its identity and raises questions with at least some about the future of the music.[41]

Other concerns arise about the increasing corporate centralization of the music in a very few large business enterprises. Part of the concern here is that corporate power is able to create and channel desire. In such a context the idea that people choose their own music is "a convenient fiction."[42] Such claims do not, however, deal with the way working people use country music to their own purposes, as I maintain above.

At the same time others are paying attention to the social and economic trends of the eighties and nineties when the rich are getting richer and the poor poorer. In a vacuum of political leadership that does not address these issues, country stars champion causes of community, charity, social justice, and humanity. They raise their voices for the environment, against homelessness and hunger, promote AIDS research, raise money for farmers, and battle nuclear power. Long-time traditions of compassion for and generosity toward those in need and others become important dimensions of the lives of a diversity of country's artists.[43]

Will White Soul Persist?

Country music has been the music of white rural working people and later those of urban America. While the music has developed a wider pop audience from time to time and especially more recently, it still contains a basic core of music "written and performed for average people."[44]

The future of the music is not, of course, clear. Probably it will become more diverse with the result that one part of the music will be aimed at and reflective of working people. Another consideration, however, is whether the bland forms of crossover country music can survive the faddish tendencies of broad popular tastes, especially if some new form should come along as did rock 'n' roll in the fifties. Whether country music can sustain itself by moving outside the social locations from which it comes and where it still holds its most durable support to date is a question that awaits the coming decades.

The future of the U.S. working class is not clear either. If present trends continue, there will be an increasing impoverishment of a significant group of working people in the society and a near-poverty status for many others, a trend that has been underway since the early seventies. The consequences of a global economy, the movement of industries to third world countries and cheap labor, the loss of good paying jobs, the continuation of national policy that endorses and supports these actions, and the emergence of an info-technological society are foreboding indeed.

So far across its history country music has, in the main, embodied white working-class life. No other music in this society that is popular with working people themselves, has been so able to sing their songs. With the country music industry hot-breathed for the crossover market, however, the future of the relationship of the music to working people could be up for grabs. My conviction and my hope is that the central core of the music will continue to be the soul music of the white working American.

Notes

Introduction: White Soul

1. Tony Scherman, "Country," *American Heritage* (November, 1994), 40.

2. Bill C. Malone, *Singing Cowboys and Musical Mountaineers: Southern Culture and Roots of Country Music* (Athens: The University of Georgia Press, 1993), 114. See Bill C. Malone, ed., *Country Music U.S.A.: A Fifty-Year History*, 1st ed. (Austin: The University of Texas Press, 1968).

3. Mary A. Bufwack and Robert K. Oermann, *Finding Her Voice: The Saga of Women in Country Music* (New York: Crown Publishers, Inc., 1993), ix.

4. Blayne Cutler, "Opportunity in Opryland," *American Demographics* (July, 1990), 45-46.

5. See Scherman, "Country," *American Heritage* (November, 1994), 57. Malone, *Country Music U.S.A.*, 359-64.

6. I am indebted here, of course, to W. E. B. DuBois, *The Souls of Black Folks* and his discussion of black soul. His point is that there is a double consciousness in the lives of African Americans. I believe that something of a parallel in consciousness occurs among white working-class people as well, only determined by class rather than race. White working-class people are profoundly conditioned by the dominant culture, but at the same time must define themselves over against that culture. For example, most white working people are very patriotic and love their country deeply. Yet, they are powerfully suspicious of the government and in no little resistance to it. This contradiction reflects both sides of a double-consciousness.

7. These are household data figures for employed persons from the U.S. Department of Labor Bureau of Labor Statistics, *Employment and Earnings* (November, 1995), 27.

8. These figures do not include farm workers. The 1990 U.S. Census reports that there are 886,000 farm workers with average median weekly incomes of $200. Of these 735,000 were males making $216 per week, and 151,000 were females with average median weekly incomes of $175. *Statistical Abstract of the United States, 1992*, 657.

Barbara Ehrenreich argues that the working class makes up 60 to 70 percent of the U.S. population. By working class she means "not only

187

industrial workers in hard hats, but all those people who are not professionals, managers, or entrepreneurs; who work for wages rather than salaries; and who spend their working hours variously lifting, bending, driving, monitoring, typing, keyboarding, cleaning, providing physical care for others, loading, unloading, cooking, serving, etc." Perhaps her definition is too broad, but it does suggest that working people remain a large group in this society, the majority in Ehrenreich's opinion. See "The Silenced Majority: Why the Average Working Person Has Disappeared from American Media and Culture," in Gail Dines and Jean M. Humez, eds., *Gender, Race, and Class in Media* (Thousand Oaks, Calif.: Sage Publications, Inc., 1995), 40-41.

9. Wallace is quoted in Sheila Collins et al., *Jobs for All: A Plan for the Revitalization of America* (New York: Council on International and Public Affairs, 1994), 16. This book is a very helpful study of the problem of employment and makes a sane case for what needs to be done. The characterization of the silent depression is drawn from pp. 16-19.

10. Bureau of Labor Statistics, "Nonfarm Payroll Statistics from the Current Employment Statistics (National) Home Page," (November 21, 1995).

11. Bureau of Labor Statistics, *Employment and Earnings*, 36.

12. See David Dembo and Ward Morehouse, *The Underbelly of the U.S. Economy: Joblessness and the Pauperization of Work in America* (New York: The Apex Press, 1994). I am indebted to a position paper prepared by Eliezer Valentin-Castanon for the General Board of Church and Society of The United Methodist Church for calling my attention to this book and this update of these unemployment figures, "Statement on Welfare" (Washington D.C.: August, 1995) mimeo., 6-7.

13. Jan Larson, "Reaching Downscale Markets," *American Demographics* (November, 1991), 39-40.

14. Patricia Braus, "One Paycheck from the Poorhouse," *American Demographics* (November, 1991), 41.

15. Barbara Ehrenreich, "Honor to the Working Stiff," *Time* (September 9, 1991), 72.

16. "Growth and Disappointment for Unions," *Kansas City Star* (September 5, 1994), B-6.

17. Bureau of Labor Statistics, "News: Usual Weekly Earnings of Wage and Salary Workers: Third Quarter 1995," 1, 3.

18. Ibid., 4.

19. Michael Harrington, "Poverty Has No Respect for Race or Gender," *Kansas City Star* (March 8, 1987), 3L.

20. See Sam Roberts, *Who We Are: A Portrait of America Today Based on the Latest United States Census* (New York: Random House, 1995), 188.

21. Jane Bryant Quinn, "A Paycheck Revolt in '96," *Newsweek* (February 19, 1996), 52.

22. John Scott Sherrill, Dennis Robbins, and Bob Dipiero, "Too Much Month at the End of the Money" (Copyright 1989 Weed Music

[ASCAP]). Recorded by Billy Hill, *Billy Hill: I Am Just a Rebel* (Copyright 1989 Reprise Records, Warner Communications Co.).

23. Pierre Bourdieu, *Distinction: A Social Critique of the Judgement of Taste,* trans. Richard Nice (Cambridge: Harvard University Press, 1984), 56-57.

PART ONE: THE POLITICS OF TASTE

Chapter 1: Rowdy and Loud at the Twist and Shout: Working-Class Taste

1. See Immanuel Kant's *Critique of Judgment,* trans. J.C. Meredith (London: Oxford University Press, 1952). My comments on Kant's views should not be taken as confirmation that he did what he set out to do. Allan McGill for example, demonstrates convincingly that while Kant argues for the autonomy of art, he can also be read as arguing for the existence of a realm of the aesthetic, a realm whose function was to mediate between the realms of nature and freedom. Moreover, while Kant denies that the aesthetic has truth value, nevertheless art seems to have the capacity to place us in contact with any number of things that are not fully available through experience or grasped by concepts, for example, art makes claims of universal validity; seems to assume a purposiveness in nature; and suggests an aesthetic view of art as giving expression to the inexpressible and as manifesting the ineffable, among others. All of these claims, of course, contend that art does have functions and hence is not autonomous. For a fuller development of these criticisms, see Allan McGill, *Prophets of Extremity: Neitzsche, Heidegger, Foucault, Derrida* (Berkeley: University of California Press, 1985), 11-13.

2. Some groups interested in art will claim otherwise because they believe that the true, the beautiful, and the good are one, but these groups might still defend the display of art on civil rights grounds.

3. Interestingly enough feminist criticisms are made of classical music because it is seen as disembodied. See Hilde Hein's "Refining Feminist Theory," in Hein and Carolyn Korsmeyer, eds., *Aesthetics in Feminist Perspective* (Bloomington: Indiana University Press, 1993), 9-13. See also Susan McClary who says that "classical music is perhaps our cultural medium most centrally concerned with denial of the body." McClary, *Feminine Endings: Music, Gender, and Sexuality* (Minneapolis: University of Minnesota Press, 1991), 79, see also 54.

4. Words by Oscar Hammerstein II and music by Richard Rodgers, "Soliloquy," *Carousel* (Copyright 1945 Williamson Music Co.).

5. Pierre Bourdieu, *Distinction: A Social Critique of the Judgement of Taste,* trans. Richard Nice (Cambridge: Harvard University Press, 1984), 34.

6. Kant, *Critique of Judgment,* 65. Quoted in Bourdieu, *Distinction,* 42. I am indebted to Bourdieu for bringing this quote to my attention.

7. Bob McDill, Wayland Holyfield, and Chuck Neese, "Rednecks, White Socks, and Blue Ribbon Beer" (Copyright 1973 Jack Music, Inc. and Jando Music, Inc.).

8. Hank Williams, Jr. "All My Rowdy Friends Are Coming Over Tonight" (Copyright 1981 Bocephus Music).

Mary Chapin Carpenter, "Down at the Twist and Shout" (Copyright 1990 EMI April Music Inc. and Getarealjob Music). About the middle-class character of Carpenter's music, Skip Hollandsworth has said "This is country that has spent some time on the analyst's couch," and reports descriptions of her music as "intellectual 'coffee house country.'" See "Sing about Her Generation," *USA Weekend* (September 24-26, 1993), 5 and 6 respectively.

Mel Tillis, "Stay Around a Little Longer" (Copyright 1982 Songs of PolyGram).

Bryan Kennedy and Jim Rushing, "American Honky-Tonk Bar Association" (Copyright 1993 EMI April Music Inc./The Old Professor's Music [ASCAP]). Recorded by Garth Brooks.

Ronnie Dunn, "Boot Scootin' Boogie" (Copyright 1989 Tree Publishing Co., admin. by Sony Music Publishing, Alfred Avenue Music [BMI]).

9. See my *Ministry in an Oral Culture: Living with Will Rogers, Uncle Remus, and Minnie Pearl* (Louisville: Westminster/John Knox Press, 1994).

10. Robin Horton, "African Traditional Thought and Western Science," *Africa* XXXVII, 1 and 2 (January and April). See section "Ideas-bound-to-occasions versus ideas-bound-to-ideas."

11. Walter J. Ong, *Orality and Literacy: The Technologizing of the World* (London: Routledge, 1982), 34.

12. Susanne K. Langer, *Philosophy in a New Key: A Study in the Symbolism of Reason, Rite and Art* (New York: A Mentor Book, 1942), 166.

13. Ibid.

14. Bourdieu, *Distinction*, 386-96.

15. Dewayne Blackwell and Bud Lee, "Friends in Low Places" (Copyright 1990 Careers Music, Inc./ Music Ridge Music, Inc. [BMI/ASCAP]). From the video *This Is Garth Brooks* (Copyright 1992 Horse of Troy Productions/A High Five Production).

16. Wayland Holyfield, "New York Wine and Tennessee Shine" (Copyright 1979 Maplehill Music & Vogue Music).

17. Bobby Goldsboro, "The Cowgirl and the Dandy" (Copyright 1977 House of Gold Music, Inc.).

18. Bourdieu, *Distinction*, 372.

19. Ibid.

20. Merle Haggard, "I Think I'll Just Stay Here and Drink" (Copyright 1980 Sony/ATV Songs LLC. All rights administered by Sony/ATV Music Publishing, 8 Music Square West, Nashville, TN 37203.)

21. John Bush Shinn, "Whiskey River" (Copyright 1972 Full Nelson Music). Recorded by Willie Nelson.

22. Bourdieu, *Distinction*, 386.

23. Carl Perkins, "Blue Suede Shoes" (Copyright 1956 Unichappell Music c/o Warner Chappell).

Chapter 2: Elitist Taste and the Politics of Aesthetics

1. Words by Otto Harbach and Oscar Hammerstein II and music by Sigmund Romberg, "The Riff Song" (Copyright 1926 Warner Bros.).

2. E. P. Thompson, *The Making of the English Working Class* (Harmondsworth: Penguin Books, 1980), 8-9.

3. Edward W. Said, *The World, the Text and the Critic* (Cambridge: Harvard University Press, 1983), 11.

4. Saussure contends that "in language there are only differences without positive terms . . . language has neither ideas nor sounds that existed before the linguistic system, but only conceptual and phonic differences that have issued from the system." Ferdinand de Saussure, *Course in General Linguistics* (London: Fontana, 1974), 120.

5. I think it is very important to make a distinction between difference and opposites. The former does not have to involve invidious comparison, but in the latter the structuring of opposites is such that the other is often "not me," or the opposite is characterized as getting its difference by being the opposite of a set of privileged categories. The result is that one's own categories or those of the privileged and powerful are determinative. They become imperial in the sense that the other is determined by being the opposite of one's own self or group definition. Hence, my criteria define the other by their oppositeness. One of the problems here as well is the tendency to project onto the other the often unacknowledged, unapproved, and unacceptable aspects of my own life. Someone has said, what we repress in ourselves we oppress in others.

6. Robert Wuthnow makes the point of how polarities open up space for discourse and introduce new arenas for public argument. See Wuthnow, *Communities of Discourse: Ideology and Social Structure in the Reformation, the Enlightenment, and European Socialism* (Cambridge: Harvard University Press, 1989), 13-14.

7. Paul Dimaggio, "Cultural Entrepreneurship in Nineteenth-Century Boston: The Creation of an Organizational Base for High Culture in America," *Media, Culture and Society*, 4, 1 (1982), 34.

8. I also realize that a position like mine can easily degenerate into supremacist claims of its own.

9. Janet Wolff, "The Ideology of Autonomous Art," in *Music and Society: The Politics of Composition, Performance, and Reception*, ed. Richard D. Leppert and Susan McClary (New York: Cambridge University Press, 1989), 5.

10. Carl Dahlhaus, *The Idea of Absolute Music*, trans. by Roger Lustig (Chicago: University of Chicago Press, 1989), 7. One should read alongside the work of Dahlhaus that of Terry Eagleton. His critique of what has happened to the aesthetic during the history of the bourgeoisie and of modernity, especially the sociopolitical sources and consequences of "autonomous art" is very helpful. See Eagleton, *The Ideology of the Aesthetic* (Oxford: Basil Blackwell, 1990). His critique of Kant, 70-101, is quite relevant here.

11. Ibid., 149.
12. Wolff in "Ideology of Autonomous Art," 10-12.
13. Susan McClary, *Feminine Endings: Music, Gender, and Sexuality* (Minneapolis: University of Minnesota Press, 1991), 3-34, 35-52, 53-79.
14. Lawrence W. Levine, *Highbrow/Lowbrow: The Emergence of Cultural Hierarchy in America* (Cambridge: Harvard University Press, 1988), 221-23.
15. Robert Walser, "Highbrow, Lowbrow, Voodoo Aesthetics," in *Microphone Fiends: Youth Music and Youth Culture*, ed. Andrew Ross and Tricia Rose (London: Routledge, 1994), 235.

PART TWO: MUSIC AS TRADITIONS

Chapter 3: Foundations, Turtles, and Music as Traditions

1. See René Descartes, *Meditations on First Philosophy* in *The Philosophical Works of Descartes*, trans. E. S. Haldane and G.R.T. Ross (Cambridge: Cambridge University Press, 1931), I, 145ff. Ludwig Wittgenstein, *On Certainty*, ed. G. E. M. Anscombe and G. H. von Wright and trans. Denis Paul and G. E. M. Anscombe (New York: Harper Torchbooks, 1969), 18e.
2. Clifford Geertz, *The Interpretation of Cultures* (New York: Basic Books, 1973), 28-29.
3. Alasdair MacIntyre, *After Virtue: A Study in Moral Theory*, 2d ed. (Notre Dame, Ind.: University of Notre Dame Press, 1984), 350-51.
4. Ibid.
5. Frank Burch Brown, *Religious Aesthetics: A Theological Study of Making and Meaning* (Princeton: Princeton University Press, 1989), 140.
6. Ibid.
7. Ibid.
8. Ibid.
9. See my *Ministry in an Oral Culture: Living with Will Rogers, Uncle Remus, and Minnie Pearl* (Louisville: Westminster/John Knox Press, 1993).
10. Melton A. McLaurin and Richard A. Peterson, *You Wrote My Life: Lyrical Themes in Country Music* (Philadelphia: Gordon and Breach, 1992), 3.
11. The music is so characterized in the title of his book *Word Movies* (Garden City, N.Y.: Doubleday, 1971), quoted in McLaurin and Peterson, *You Wrote My Life*, 2.
12. Tom T. Hall, "Harper Valley P.T.A." (Copyright 1967 Newkeys Music. Copyright assigned to Unichappell Music, Inc. and Morris Music, Inc.). In this connection a semiotic analysis of country music would make a significant contribution to the study of the genre. Let me be clear that I am not suggesting some ideal "essence." These signs express rather the conventions developed over the course of its history as a tradition.

13. Dorothy Horstman, *Sing Your Heart Out, Country Boy* (Nashville: Vanderbilt University Press, 1995), xix.

14. Waylon Jennings, "Are You Sure Hank Done It This Way?" (Copyright 1975 Hall-Clement Publication [c/o The Welk Group]).

15. The roots of commercial country music go back much further than a hundred years. See Bill C. Malone, *Country Music U.S.A.: A Fifty-Year History* (Austin: University of Texas Press, 1968), chap. 1; see also Mary A. Bufwack and Robert K. Oermann, *Finding Her Voice: The Saga of Women in Country Music* (New York: Crown Publishers, Inc., 1993), chap. 1.

16. Alasdair MacIntyre, *Whose Justice? Which Rationality?* (Notre Dame, Ind.: University of Notre Dame Press, 1989), 390.

17. Ludwig Wittgenstein, *The Blue and Brown Books*, 2d ed. (New York: Harper Torchbooks, 1960), 17-19.

Chapter 4: You Wrote My Life: The Goods of Country Music

1. I am obviously making a play here on Wittgenstein's notion of language as language in use. See his discussion of language games in *The Blue and Brown Books*, 80-81.

2. Charles F. Gritzner, "Country Music: A Reflection of Popular Culture," *Journal of Popular Culture, II* (1978), 860.

3. Quoted in Bill C. Malone, *Country Music U.S.A.: A Fifty-Year History* (Austin: University of Texas Press, 1968), 237.

4. Dorothy Horstman, *Sing Your Heart Out, Country Boy* (Nashville: Vanderbilt University Press, 1995), xix-xx.

5. Quoted in John Buckley, "Tom T. Hall: Country Music and American Values," *Popular Music and Society*, 295.

6. Unpublished interview with Robert K. Oermann, March 2, 1992, Nashville. Quoted in Mary A. Bufwack, "Girls with Guitars—and Fringe and Sequins and Rhinestones, Silk, Lace, and Leather," in *Readin' Country Music: Steel Guitars, Opry Stars, and Honky Tonk Bars*, a special issue of *The South Atlantic Quarterly*, ed. Cecelia Tichi (Winter 1995) 94, 1, 216. Italics mine.

7. Bufwack, "Girls with Guitars," 208.

8. Richard Hoggart, *The Uses of Literacy* (New Brunswick, N.J.: Transaction Publishers, 1991), 238, 120. The problem with Hoggart's work is his tendency to see working-class life as now corrupted by the commercialization and mass culture of late capitalism. He fails to see that working people are not simply reflectors of mass culture, and does not follow his own best thought in noting the ways they use mass culture. They are not stooges, and can use it to their own ends. We shall see this in even more detail in subsequent chapters.

9. A very fruitful direction for working on the response of working people to popular culture is Ien Ang, *Watching Dallas: Soap Opera and the Melodramatic Imagination* (London: Methuen, 1985). It is this more complex rendering of the dynamics of "ordinary" people using popular culture that we need. Her work has helped me in thinking through the use

of country music by working people. For a position critical of Ang see Dana Polan, "Complexity and Contradiction in Mass-Culture Analysis: On Ien Ang Watching Dallas," *Camera Obscura*, 16 (Winter, 1988).

10. Quoted in Horstman, *Sing Your Heart Out*, 145. Malone's comment about Pierce is from *Stars of Country Music*, ed. Bill C. Malone and Judith McColluh (New York: Da Capo, 1991), 412.

11. Arlie R. Hochschild, *The Managed Heart: Commercialization of Human Feeling* (Berkeley: University of California Press, 1983), 172-73.

PART THREE: THE CONTRADICTIONS AND THE POLITICS OF RESISTANCE IN COUNTRY MUSIC

Chapter 5: Tradition, Modernity, and the Wild Side of Life

1. Anthony Giddens, a British sociologist, defines contradiction as "the existence of two structural principles within a societal system, whereby each depends upon the other but at the same time negates it." These contradictions involve both "the fusion and exclusion of opposites." That is, the operation of one structural characteristic involves that of another which tends to undermine it. *A Contemporary Critique of Historical Materialism* (Berkeley: University of California Press, 1981), 231.

2. Bob McDill and Dan Seals, "Five Generations of Rock County Wilsons" (Copyright 1988 PolyGram International Publishing, Inc./Ranger Bob Music/Pink Pig Music).

3. See especially Wendell Berry, *Home Economics* (New York: North Point Press—Farrar, Straus and Giroux, 1987) and *Sex, Economy, Freedom and Community: Eight Essays* (New York: Pantheon Books, 1992).

4. Dolly Parton, "In the Good Old Days" (Copyright 1968 Velvet Apple Music c/o Gelfland, Rennert and Feldman).

5. Bob McDill and Dan Seals, "They Rage On" (Copyright 1988 Poly-Gram International Publishing, Inc./Ranger Bob Music/Pink Pig Music).

6. Chris Waters and Chuck Jones, "Cadillac Ranch" (Copyright 1991 Great Cumberland Music [BMI]/Diamond Struck Music [BMI]). Recorded by Chris LeDoux.

7. I realize that I am not addressing other issues like working-class taste for festivity and "letting it all hang out," but this does not seem to be the focus of this song. I see it as a critique of modernity, not a working-class form of resistance.

8. See the critique of modernity in Alasdair MacIntyre, *After Virtue: A Study in Moral Theory*, 2d ed. (Notre Dame, Ind.: University of Notre Dame Press, 1984), 250-55. From a theological perspective see Stanley Hauerwas, *Dispatches from the Front: Theological Engagements with the Secular* (Durham: Duke University Press, 1994), part II.

9. Walter J. Ong, *Orality and Literacy: The Technologizing of the World* (London: Routledge, 1982), 48.

10. Giddens, *Contemporary Critique*, 251.

11. In a very real sense the music "tells it like it is." But even this is contested by some thinkers. Peterson and McLaurin contend that music, "whether country or any other genre," does "not reflect all that is on people's minds, and thus cannot be read as a complete assessment of the collective consciousness of the country music audience." (See Melton A. McLaurin and Richard A. Peterson, *You Wrote My Life: Lyrical Themes in Country Music* [Philadelphia: Gordon and Breach, 1992], 6.) These two authors make a spectacular claim when they say: "While country music, from the perspective of its audience, may be said to tell nothing but the truth, it does not tell the *whole* truth that might be discovered in an investigation made by a sociologist, historian, psychologist, or anthropologist," p. 8. (Italics in the original.) I would like to know the name of *any* sociologist, historian, psychologist, or anthropologist, who tells the whole truth. This McLaurin and Peterson comment is not relieved by their use of the word "might." This is precisely the kind of academic self-elevation that leads many people to so distrust us. I do not know any discipline—certainly not the human "sciences"—that reflects "all that is on people's minds."

Further, country music is an art form and a poetry. It is not supposed to be exact in any discursive sense. As Durkheim says there is no fully reflective art, meaning that art always outruns the ideas at work to understand it. I never hear people complain that Van Gogh's trees do not look like "real trees" or that Picasso's people do not look like people on the street.

To say that country music "tells it like it is" does not mean some exact replication of working-class attitudes. It is not an edited set of field notes like those of an anthropologist. It is not a case study, or the transcription of an interview. It is not any of these (thank goodness), rather it is an artistic and poetic, sometimes an overweening commercial one, attempt to put in song some dimension of life. When it does such songs in story I believe it can come closer to working-class life than theory can. See John Milbank, *Theology and Social Theory: Beyond Secular Reason* (London: Basil Blackwell Ltd., 1990), 380-88.

12. Jimmie Rodgers, "T for Texas" ("Blue Yodel") (Copyright 1928 Peer International Corporation). Copyright renewed.

13. Michael Bane, quoted in Joli Kathleen Jensen, "Creating the Nashville Sound: A Case Study in Commercial Culture Production," Ph.D. diss., University of Illinois at Urbana-Champagne, 1984, 68.

14. Rebecca Klatch, "Coalition and Conflict among Women of the New Right," *Signs* 13, 4 (1988): 675-76.

15. See my discussion of these issues in *Blue Collar Ministry* (Valley Forge, Pa.: Judson Press, 1984), 71-83, and *U.S. Lifestyles and Mainline Churches* (Philadelphia: Westminster/John Knox Press, 1990), 59-60.

16. Arlie Hochschild and Anne Machung, *The Second Shift* (New York: Avon Books, 1990).

17. William Warren and Arlie Carter, "The Wild Side of Life" (Copy-

right 1952 EMI Publishing). Recorded by Hank Thompson. J. D. Miller, "It Wasn't God Who Made Honky Tonk Angels" (Copyright 1952 APRS). Recorded by Kitty Wells.

18. John Bush Shinn, "Whiskey River" (Copyright 1972 Full Nelson Music). Recorded by Willie Nelson. Tommy Duncan, Cindy Walker, and Bob Wills, "Bubbles in My Beer," (Copyright Bob Wills Music, Inc. and Red River Songs, Inc. Copyright renewed by Unichappell Music, Inc. [Rightsong Music, Publishers]).

Lorene Allen, Don McHan, and T. D. Bayless, "The Pill," (Copyright 1973 and 1975 Coal Miners Music, Inc. and Guaranty Music Inc.).

Mel Tillis, "Ruby, Don't Take Your Love to Town," (Copyright 1966 Cedarwood Publishing Co.).

19. Jim Ault, "Family and Fundamentalism: The Shawmut Valley Baptist Church," in *Disciplines of Faith*, ed. Jim Obelkevich and Lyndal Roper (London: Routledge & Kegan Paul, 1987), 13-36.

20. Dorothy Horstman, *Sing Your Heart Out, Country Boy* (Nashville: Vanderbilt University Press, 1995), 213. Lefty Frizzell and Jim Beck, "If You've Got the Money I've Got the Time" (Copyright 1950 Peer Southern Organization).

21. One should not miss the considerable resistance to the dominant order to be found in country music in general and honky-tonk music especially, but we shall turn to that in a subsequent chapter.

Chapter 6: Defiance, Love, Gender, and Race

1. David Allan Coe, "Take This Job and Shove It" (Copyright 1977 Warner-Tamerlane Publishing Corp.). Recorded by Johnny Paycheck.

2. Merle Travis, "Sixteen Tons" (Copyright 1947 American Music, Inc. Copyright assigned to Unichappell Music, Inc. [Rightsong Music, Publisher] and Elvis Presley Music). Recorded by Tennessee Ernie Ford.

3. Dolly Parton, "9 to 5" (Copyright 1980 Velvet Apple Music and Fox Fanfare Music, Inc.).

4. Jimmie N. Rogers, *The Country Music Message Revisited* (Fayetteville: University of Arkansas Press, 1988), 11.

5. Elvis Presley, "All Shook Up" (Copyright R & H Music). Dolly Parton, "Great Balls of Fire" (Copyright 1957 by Hill and Range Songs, Inc.). Originally performed by Jerry Lee Lewis.

6. Laurie Lewis, "Love Chooses You" (Copyright 1987 Spruce and Maple Music [Admin. by Forerunner Music Inc.]/Forerunner Music Inc. [ASCAP]). Recorded by Kathy Mattea.

7. Jon Vezner and Don Henry, "Where've You Been" (Copyright 1988 Wrensong Publishing Corp./Cross Keys Publishing Co. Inc./Tree Group). Recorded by Kathy Mattea. Jon Vezner tells an interesting story about this song. He wrote it about his grandparents. When he tried to pitch it to music publishers on Music Row, no one wanted to touch it. "Who wants to hear about old people in a nursing home?" they said. Vezner was able to get Kathy Mattea (his wife) to record the song, and it

went on to become Song of the Year. (Jon Vezner, speaking at a Tennessee Songwriters Association workshop, Gallatin, Tennessee, January, 1991.)

8. Quoted in Curtis W. Ellison, *Country Music Culture: From Hard Times to Heaven* (University Press of Mississippi, 1995), 245.

9. For Reba's quote see Mary A. Bufwack and Robert K. Oermann, *Finding Her Voice: The Saga of Women in Country Music* (New York: Crown Publishers, Inc., 1993), 534. For Loretta's see Frye Gaillard, *Watermelon Wine* (New York: St. Martin's Press, 1978), xiv. For the Rogers's quote about Dottie see also Bufwack and Oermann, *Finding Her Voice*, 164.

10. Larry Gatlin, "Statues Without Hearts" (Copyright 1976 First Generation Music c/o EMI Blackwood).

11. The Gallup Report, *Religion in America*, No. 222 (Princeton: The Princeton Religion Research Center, Inc., 1984), 5.

12. See William Valentine, *Culture and Poverty* (Chicago: University of Chicago, 1968); Beth E. Vanfossen, *The Structure of Social Inequality* (Boston: Little, Brown and Company, 1979), 324-45; Michael B. Katz, *The Undeserving Poor: From the War on Poverty to the War on Welfare* (New York: Pantheon Books, 1989), 36-78. For a recent confirmation of this finding see Sam Roberts, *Who We Are: A Portrait of America Today Based on the Latest United States Census* (New York: Random House, 1995), 51.

13. Ellison, *Country Music Culture*, 118-19.

14. Dallas Frazier, "There Goes My Everything" (Copyright 1965, 1966 Acuff-Rose-Opryland Music, Inc. and Husky Music, Inc.).

15. Johnny Paycheck, "All-American Man" (Copyright 1975 EMI Algee Music Corp.).

16. Bufwack and Oermann report that in 1990 "the hunk period" drops women artists to 12 percent on the charts after having been 25 to 35 percent of the charts. See Bufwack and Oermann, *Finding Her Voice*, 530.

17. Peter Guralnick, *Last Train to Memphis: The Rise of Elvis Presley* (Boston: Little, 1994), 426.

18. Gaillard, *Watermelon Wine*, 92.

19. Melton A. McLaurin and Richard A. Peterson, *You Wrote My Life: Lyrical Themes in Country Music* (Philadelphia: Gordon and Breach, 1992), 7.

20. Tom T. Hall, "I Want to See the Parade" (Copyright Unichappel-New Key Music).

21. "Irma Jackson" (Copyright Tree Publishing). Recorded by Merle Haggard. Bobby Braddock, "I Believe the South Is Gonna Rise Again" (Copyright Tree Publishing). Recorded by Tanya Tucker.

22. Bufwack and Oermann, *Finding Her Voice*, 328.

23. McLaurin and Peterson, *You Wrote My Life*, 54-55.

Chapter 7: Country Music and the Politics of Resistance

1. Pierre Bourdieu, *Language and Symbolic Power* (Cambridge: Harvard University Press, 1991), 88.

2. Curtis W. Ellison, *Country Music Culture: From Hard Times to Heaven* (University Press of Mississippi, 1995), 10.

3. Dorothy Horstman, *Sing Your Heart Out, Country Boy* (Nashville: Vanderbilt University Press, 1995), 96.

4. Jimmie N. Rogers, *The Country Music Message Revisited* (Fayetteville: University of Arkansas Press, 1988), 17, 34, 64, 89, and 90.

5. Margaret Jones, *Patsy: The Life and Times of Patsy Cline* (New York: HarperCollins, 1994), 230-32.

6. John Fiske, *Television Culture: Popular Pleasures and Politics* (London: Routledge, 1988), 316. See also his *Understanding Popular Culture* (London: Unwin Hyman, 1989), 20-21.

7. Kris Kristofferson, "Third World Warrior" (Copyright 1990 Polygram Records, Inc.).

8. See Barbara Ehrenreich, *Fear of Falling: The Inner Life of the Middle Class* (New York: Harper Perennial, 1989), 124-27. Richard F. Hamilton, *Class and Politics in the United States* (New York: Wiley, 1972), 399-506.

9. Fiske, *Understanding Popular Culture*, 8, 20-21.

10. Bill C. Malone and Judith McCulloh, eds., *Stars of Country Music*, 1st ed. (New York: Da Capo, 1991), 442-43. See also Bill C. Malone, *Country Music U.S.A.: A Fifty-Year History* (Austin: University of Texas Press, 1968), 278.

11. Ellison, *Country Music Culture*, 137.

12. Mikhail Bakhtin, *Rabelais and His World*, trans. Helene Iswolsky (Bloomington: Indiana University Press, 1984), 271.

13. Ibid., 196-277.

14. Bryan Kennedy and Jim Rushing, "American Honky-Tonk Bar Association" (Copyright 1993 EMI April Music Inc./The Old Professor's Music). Recorded by Garth Brooks.

15. Fiske, *Understanding Popular Culture*, 20-21.

16. Michel de Certeau, *The Practice of Everyday Life*, trans. Steven F. Rendall (Berkeley: University of California Press, 1984), 37, 40.

17. Ellison, *Country Music Culture*, 140.

18. Jacques Attali, *Noise: The Political Economy of Music*, trans. Brian Massumi (Minneapolis: University of Minnesota Press, 1985), 8.

19. Lillian B. Bubin, *Worlds of Pain: Life in the Working Class Family* (New York: Basic Books, Inc., 1992), 159.

20. Walter Brueggemann, *The Prophetic Imagination* (Philadelphia: Fortress Press, 1978), 44-61, esp. 60.

21. Merle Haggard, "If We Make It Through December" (Copyright 1973 Shade Tree Music).

22. Mary A. Bufwack and Robert K. Oermann, *Finding Her Voice: The Saga of Women in Country Music* (New York: Crown Publishers, Inc., 1993), 248.

23. Quoted in ibid., 249.

24. de Certeau, *The Practice of Everyday Life*, 41.

25. Bufwack and Oermann, *Finding Her Voice*, 248.

26. William Warren and Arlie Carter, "The Wild Side of Life" (Copyright 1952 EMI Publishing). Recorded by Hank Thompson.

27. J. D. Miller, "It Wasn't God Who Made Honky Tonk Angels" (Copyright 1952 APRS). Recorded by Kitty Wells.

28. Bufwack and Oermann, *Finding Her Voice*, 178-79.

29. This hasn't changed much. The casual listener will discover, that, on average, for every ten consecutive songs played on country music radio stations, eight are usually male artists (or groups) and two are female artists (but rarely played back to back).

30. Ellison, *Country Music Culture*, 180.

31. Don Cusic, *Reba: Country Music's Queen* (New York: St. Martin's Press, 1993), 154. One relatively new female artist, Martina McBride, has had great success with her release of the song, "Independence Day," which focuses on domestic violence, and one woman's very drastic response to it. It is a very empowering song for women, although for some people, it may be considered controversial.

Chapter 8: Traditional Politics and Populist Anarchism

1. Dorothy Horstman, *Sing Your Heart Out, Country Boy* (Nashville: Vanderbilt University Press, 1995), 231.

2. Ibid.

3. Ibid.

4. Merle Haggard and Roy Edward Burris, "Okie from Muskogee" (Copyright 1969 Tree Publishing).

5. Quoted in Horstman, *Sing Your Heart Out*, 240.

6. Merle Haggard, "The Fightin' Side of Me" (Copyright 1970 Tree Publishing).

7. Bill Malone, *The Smithsonian Collection of Classic Country Music*, selected and annotated by Bill C. Malone (Washington D.C.: The Smithsonian Institution, 1981), 20.

8. Merle Haggard, "Hungry Eyes" (Copyright 1969, 1971 Tree Publishing Inc.).

9. James Ring Adams, "Musical Great Awakening: Country's New Traditionalists," *Policy Review* (Fall, 1987), 77.

10. Tony Scherman, "Country," *American Heritage* (November, 1994), 52.

11. I address these issues in my *U.S. Lifestyles and Mainline Churches* (Louisville: Westminster/John Knox Press, 1990.) See the section on the cultural right.

12. Hank Williams, Jr., "A Country Boy Can Survive" (Copyright 1981 Bocephus Music Co.). Dwight Yoakam, "Readin', Rightin', Rt. 23" (Copyright 1987 Coal Dust West Music).

13. Mary Chapin Carpenter, "I Am a Town" (Copyright 1992 EMI AprilMusic, Inc./Getarealjob Music).

14. Johnny Cash, "One Piece at a Time" (Copyright 1976 Columbia Records).

15. Kostal, "Lord Have Mercy on the Working Man" (Copyright 1990 Songs of Polygram International). Recorded by Travis Tritt.

16. Jerry Chestnut, "Oney" (Copyright 1972 Passkey Music, Inc.).

17. Horstman, *Sing Your Heart Out*, 255.

18. Ibid., 256.

19. Billy Joe Shaver, "Old Five and Dimers (Like Me)" (Copyright 1972 ATV Music Corp.).

20. Bill Anderson, "Po' Folks" (Copyright 1961 Tree Publishing Co.).

21. Jack Moran and Glenn Tubb, "Skip a Rope" (Copyright 1967 Tree Publishing Co.).

22. "Put Another Log on the Fire" (Copyright 1975 MGM Records). Recorded by Tompall Glaser.

PART FOUR: THE IMPLICATIONS FOR THE CHURCH

Chapter 9: The Church as a Community of Resistance

1. Roger Cook and Sam Hogin, "I Believe in You" (Copyright 1980 Roger Cook Music and Cookhouse Music).

2. Billy Sherrill and Glenn Sutton, "The Outlaw's Prayer" (Copyright 1978 Julep Publishing Co. and Flagship Music, Inc.).

3. See Roger M. Williams, *Sing a Sad Song: The Life of Hank Williams*, 2nd ed. (Champaign: University of Illinois Press, 1981), 160-61. See also Curtis W. Ellison, *Country Music Culture: From Hard Times to Heaven* (University Press of Mississippi, 1995), 111. Ellison reports that 15 percent of Hank's songs were gospel and religious songs.

4. Chet Flippo, *Your Cheatin' Heart* (New York: St. Martin's Press, 1993), 49. See also Christopher Metress, "Sing Me a Song about a Ramblin' Man," in *Readin' Country Music: Steel Guitars, Opry Stars, and Honky Tonk Bars*, a special issue of *The South Atlantic Quarterly*, ed. Cecelia Tichi (Winter 1995) 94, 1, 24. I am indebted to Metress for bringing this comment to my attention.

5. About this gap between spirituality and institutional religion especially among baby boomers see Wade Clark Roof, *A Generation of Seekers: The Spiritual Journeys of the Baby Boom Generation* (San Francisco: Harper, 1993), 78-79.

6. Tom T. Hall, "Me and Jesus" (Copyright 1972 Hallnote Music, admin. by Unichappell Music Inc.).

7. David Sanjek, "Blue Moon of Kentucky Rising," *Readin' Country Music*, 44-45. This is in reference to the work of W. J. Cash, *The Mind of the South* (New York: Doubleday Anchor Books, 1954), 65-70.

8. Antonio de Nebrija, *Gramatica de la lengua castellana*, ed. Ig. Gonzalez Llubera (Oxford, 1926), 3; Lewis Hanke, *Aristotle and the American Indians: A Study in Race Prejudice in the Modern World* (Chicago and London: 1959), 8. Quoted in Stephen J. Greenblatt, *Learning to Curse: Essays in Early Modern Culture* (New York: Routledge, 1990), 16-17.

9. Pierre Bourdieu, *Language and Symbolic Power* (Cambridge: Harvard University Press, 1991), 88.

10. I am pleased to note that country music is doing more with issues of social justice and a range of social issues. See Mary A. Bufwack and Robert K. Oermann, *Finding Her Voice: The Saga of Women in Country Music* (New York: Crown Publishers, Inc., 1993), 537.

Chapter 10: The "Trashy" Church

1. I am deeply indebted to Steven D. Hoogerwerf in this chapter. His dissertation on the place resistance can play in the church so that it can "sing the Lord's song in a strange land" is a fine piece of work. He will perhaps not be pleased with my combination of his work with the conviction that the redemptive work of the Spirit is found in the indigenous practices of working people and country music. Certainly one should not take my statements here as indicative of his position. It clearly deserves a careful reading of its own. See "Forming the Character of Christian Discipleship: Singing the Lord's Song in a Strange Land," Ph.D. diss., Duke University, 1991, 315-16. I am indebted to this dissertation for its helpful discussion of "everyday resistance" (see chapter 7). I appreciate Stanley Hauerwas's recommendation of it to me.

2. John Masefield quoted in Robert C. Solomon, *In the Spirit of Hegel* (New York: Oxford University Press, 1983), 231.

3. See my *U.S. Lifestyles and Mainline Churches* (Louisville: Westminster/John Knox Press, 1990), 74-76.

4. I address these issues in more detail in *Blue Collar Ministry* (Valley Forge, Pa.: Judson Press, 1984), 21-32, 119-24.

5. See Hoogerwerf on this point, "Forming the Character of Christian Discipleship," 1-2, 159-79.

6. See my *Ministry in An Oral Culture: Living with Will Rogers, Uncle Remus, and Minnie Pearl* (Louisville: Westminster/John Knox Press, 1993), 73-94.

Chapter 11: Doing Theology with Country Music

1. Kris Kristofferson, "Help Me Make It Through the Night" (Copyright 1970 Combine Music Co.). Recorded by Sammi Smith.

2. Albert Outler, *Evangelism in the Wesleyan Spirit* (Nashville: Tidings, 1971), 98.

3. Kristofferson, "Help Me Make It Through the Night."

4. Dolly Parton, "Coat of Many Colors" (Copyright 1969 Velvet Apple Music, Inc.). Recorded by Dolly Parton.

5. Curtis W. Ellison, *Country Music Culture: From Hard Times to Heaven* (University Press of Mississippi, 1995), 164.

6. Ray Stevens, "The Mississippi Squirrel Revival" (Copyright 1984, MCA Records). Note I am making use of an earlier paper of mine in this chapter: "Country Music as a Resource for Lenten Preaching," *Journal for Preachers*, XVI, 2 (Lent, 1993), 9.

7. Quoted in Ellison, *Country Music Culture*, 164.

8. Larry Gatlin, "The Midnight Choir" (Copyright 1977 Combine

Music c/o EMI Blackwood). Recorded by Larry Gatlin and the Gatlin Brothers.

9. I am indebted to David Bennett for this characterization of hard living.

Appendix: A'Pickin' and A'Sangin': A Short History of Country Music

1. Bill C. Malone, *Singing Cowboys and Musical Mountaineers* (Athens: University of Georgia Press, 1993), 114.

2. Ibid., 115.

3. Bill Malone, *The Smithsonian Collection of Classic Country Music*, selected and annotated by Bill C. Malone (Washington D.C.: The Smithsonian Institution, 1981), 5. I have used this briefer history of his in the *Smithsonian Collection* as a way to focus on the most important events in the history of the music. His longer work, *Country Music U.S.A.: A Fifty-Year History* (Austin: University of Texas Press, 1968), however, provides richer detail. Both deserve a careful reading.

4. Malone, *Country Music U.S.A.*, 216.

5. Malone, *The Smithsonian Collection*, 6.

6. Mary A. Bufwack and Robert K. Oermann, *Finding Her Voice: The Saga of Women in Country Music* (New York: Crown Publishers, Inc., 1993), x.

7. James K. Morris, introductory comments in *The Smithsonian Collection*, 2.

8. Bob Millard, *Country Music: 70 Years of America's Favorite Music* (New York: HarperCollins, 1993), 30.

9. Malone, *The Smithsonian Collection*, 6.

10. Ibid.

11. Ibid.

12. Ibid.

13. U.S. Department of Commerce and Bureau of the Census, *Historical Statistics of the United States: Colonial Times to 1970* (White Plains, New York: Kraus International Publications, 1989), 457.

14. U.S. Bureau of the Census, *Statistical Abstract of the United States: 1992* (112th edition), Washington, D.C., 1992, 643.

15. Bufwack and Oermann, *Finding Her Voice*, 113-15.

16. Ibid., 81.

17. Malone, *Singing Cowboys and Musical Mountaineers*, 71-74.

18. Malone, *The Smithsonian Collection*, 8.

19. Ibid., 9.

20. Malone, *Country Music U.S.A.*, 206.

21. Bufwack and Oermann, *Finding Her Voice*, 142-44.

22. Daniel Yankelovich, *New Rules: Searching for Self-Fulfillment in a World Turned Upside Down* (New York: Random House, 1981), 21. See also Judith Stacey, *Brave New Families: Stories of Domestic Upheaval in Late Twentieth Century America* (New York: Basic Books, 1991), 8-12.

23. Malone, *The Smithsonian Collection*, 11.

24. Ibid.

25. Ibid.

26. Ibid., 14.

27. See Margaret Jones' fine biography *Patsy: The Life and Times of Patsy Cline* (New York: HarperCollins, 1994).

28. Malone, *The Smithsonian Collection*, 16.

29. Malone, *Country Music U.S.A.*, 273.

30. Ibid., 276.

31. Ibid., 319.

32. Ibid., 306-16.

33. Ibid., 308-10.

34. Ibid., 317-21.

35. Ibid., 373-75.

36. Ibid., 405.

37. Bufwack and Oermann, *Finding Her Voice*, 304-25.

38. Tony Scherman, "Country," *American Heritage* (November, 1994), 55.

39. Blayne Cutler, "Opportunity in Opryland," *American Demographics* (July 1990), 45-46.

40. Scherman, "Country," 54. One hardly needs to agree with Scherman on his views about artists like Dolly to be concerned about the popularization of country music and the potentiality with that of losing its close connection with working people.

41. Ibid.

42. Ibid., 57.

43. Bufwack and Oermann, *Finding Her Voice*, 537-38.

44. Morris, quoted in *The Smithsonian Collection*, 2.

Index

absolute music, 49, 51
Academy of Country Music Awards, 71
Acuff, Roy, 74, 180
aesthetic(s), 28-31, 32-34, 38-40, 53
   dominated, 34-39, 75; essence, 66;
   Kant's, 38-39
African Americans, 22, 106-108; influence, 107, 177
Alabama, 183
"All My Rowdy Friends Are Coming Over Tonight," 115
"All Shook Up," 100
Allen, Rex, 179
American Civil Liberties Union, 126
"American Honky-Tonk Bar Association," 32, 115
anarchism, populist, 22, 124-28, 151-52
Anderson, Bill, 183
Anderson, John, 184
"Are You Sure Hank Done It This Way," 65
artistic, the, 67
Atkins, Chet, 181
Ault, Jim, 95
Autry, Gene, 179, 180
autonomy of the arts, 48-49, 50

Bailey, Deford, 107, 183
Bakhtin, Mikhail, 115
Bandy, Moe, 184
beating the system, 130-31
beauty, 66-67
"Before the Next Teardrop Falls," 102
"Behind Closed Doors," 100
Black, Clint, 185
"Blue Bayou," 102

"Blue Moon of Kentucky," 181
"Blue Suede Shoes," 37, 38
"Blue Yodel," 91
bluegrass, 63, 182, 183
"Boot Scootin' Boogie," 32
Bourdieu, Pierre, 21, 34, 35, 76, 110, 144
"Born to Lose," 82, 92, 180
Brooks, Garth, 32, 34-35, 74, 92, 104, 115, 185
Brown, Frank Burch, 62-63
Bruce, Ed, 184
"Bubbles in My Beer," 94
Bufwack, Mary A., 13, 118, 177
Butcher Hollow, 34, 120

"Cadillac Ranch," 89-90
Campbell, Glenn, 182
Campbell, Will, 64
Carnegie Hall, 112, 118
Carpenter, Mary Chapin, 31, 129, 185
Carson, Fiddlin' John, 176
Carter, A. P. (family), 65, 178
Cash, Johnny, 130, 182
church, 137-52, 153-62
Civil Rights movement, 27, 107, 183
Clark, Roy, 77
class, 16-20, 42-47, 44-45; captivities of, 142-46; in the arts, 50-51; in the church, 13, 52, 142-46
classism, 50, 105, 166
Cline, Patsy, 62, 74, 104, 112, 116, 119-20, 182, 183
Clower, Jerry, 168-69
"Coal Miner's Daughter," 129
"Coat of Many Colors," 129
"Cold, Cold Heart," 102
Colter, Jessi, 184